Dictionary of the Cruise Industry

Terms used in cruise industry
management • operations • law
finance • marketing
ship design and construction

Giora Israel
and
Laurence Miller

A
Seatrade
CRUISE ACADEMY
PUBLICATION

First edition 1999

Published by Seatrade Cruise Academy
Seatrade House
42 North Station Road
Colchester CO1 1RB, UK
Tel +44 1206 545121
Fax +44 1206 545190
e-mail 100125.543@compuserve.com

© Giora Israel and Laurence Miller 1999

Although every effort has been made to ensure that the information contained in this publication is correct, the authors and publishers accept no liability for errors that may occur. All rights reserved. No part of this publication may be reproduced, stored in a retrieval system or transmitted in any form without the prior written permission of the copyright owner and publisher.

ISBN 0-905597-70-2

Printed in the UK by Lavenham Press
Designed by Caroline McCann and David Andrews
Illustrated by Jerry Hoare

INTRODUCTION

This publication is intended to be a guide to terms used commonly in the cruise industry: in management, marketing, operations, and in the design and construction of cruise ships. Where appropriate, definitions go beyond simple meanings to convey some of the history and lore of cruising and ocean travel.

In the days when the cruise industry was small and its people mainly drawn from shipping companies, a work such as this was, perhaps, little needed. However, as the 1990's give way to the new millennium, the industry is expanding rapidly and gaining strength as well as new middle and senior management from allied industries ashore. It is the hope of the authors that the many individuals newly associated with the cruise industry, and others seeking to join or to do business with it, will find this book useful and, perhaps, gain a sense of the indistry's traditions.

While cruising is an increasingly big business concerned with marketing and yields, it is still in a major way an enterprise of those who make their living from the sea and ships. In spite of what it has in common with the hospitality industry and its dependence, new and traditional, on those who work in many shoreside occupations from banking to transportation, the cruise industry is different and involved in no small way in man's relationship with the sea.

Many have contributed to the compilation of this book. First, the authors would like to express their thanks to the Advisory Board who have taken the time to read the manuscript and offer their advice. Their names are listed on the following page. The help they have given has been invaluable. Among other assistance, they have worked to ensure that the definitions in this book reflect the culture not

Introduction

of one company but of many. However, the authors would like to emphasize that the Advisory Board is not responsible for any errors or omissions. The creators of this dictionary have had to make the final decisions on all definitions.

Others have rendered assistance in many ways and are deserving of mention. In the Carnival Corporation, these include Susana M. Brid, Larry Friedman, Alberto Garcia, William J. Green, John Klein, Enrique Miguez, Thomas Thamason, and J.C. Trueba; at Florida International University, Jan DeCarlo and Mayra Fernandez; at Seatrade, Ken Burgess; and at home, our wives Denise Israel and Carole Miller for their understanding, patience, and help with the critique of this work.

Giora Israel   **Laurence Miller**
January 4, 1999

ADVISORY BOARD

Ernest Blum
  Southeast Bureau Chief Associate, Travel Weekly

Cynthia Colenda
  President, International Council of Cruise Lines (ICCL)

Roberto Giorgi
  Managing Director, V-Ships

James Godsman
  President, Cruise Lines International Association (CLIA)

Johan Groothuizen
  Director, Hotel & Marine Operations, Holland America Line

Christopher Hayman
  Managing Director, Seatrade

Lawrence Kaye
  Partner, Kaye Rose & Partners

Brian E. Major
  Senior Cruise Editor, Travel Agent Magazine

Stephen A. Nielsen
  Vice President, Caribbean Affairs & Operations, Princess Cruises

Roderick McLeod
  Senior Vice President, Marketing, Carnival Corporation

Stephen Payne
  Senior Naval Architect and Project Coordinator, Carnival Corporation Technical Services U.K.

Dictionary of the Cruise Industry

About the Authors

From left: Laurence Miller and Giora Israel

Giora Israel, Vice President Strategic Planning, Carnival Corporation, is a veteran of both the hotel and cruise industries at senior levels. A graduate of Tadmore Hotel College in Herzliah, Israel, he served as Director of Sales and Marketing at the Tel Aviv Hilton and as general manager of hotels in Israel and in The Bahamas. He also managed two marine parks and underwater observatories in The Bahamas and in St. Thomas, US Virgin Islands, before becoming a cruise industry consultant in 1989. In 1992, he joined Carnival Corporation as Director of Special Projects, where he engaged in a variety of international activities for the line in Europe and in other parts of the world. This included an assignment to Greece as Senior Vice President of Epirotiki during the Carnival/Epirotiki joint venture. In his present position, Mr Israel is involved with Carnival's international expansion. Other responsibilities include strategic developments relating to ports and other areas. All these have endowed him with an insider's broad perspective of the cruise industry.

About the Authors

Dr Laurence Miller, Executive Director of Libraries, Florida International University in Miami, received his Ph.D from Florida State University. A lifelong lover of ships and the sea, he has written widely over the past twenty years for newspapers, journals, and magazines in North America and in U.K. He regularly writes ship profiles for *Travel Agent Magazine*, articles for *Cruise Travel Magazine*, and has served as contributor of cruise ship and cruise line evaluations to *Fodor's Worldwide Cruises and Ports of Call*. At Florida International University, Dr Miller lectures on cruise line management for the School of Hospitality Management and writes regularly for the School's *FIU Hospitality Review*. He has been an interested and well-known observer of the passenger shipping industry during its critical period of transformation from line voyages to cruises.

USER SUGGESTIONS

The authors have tried to make this publication as comprehensive as possible. If you, the reader, believe a word widely used and relevant to the publication has been omitted, or if you would like to suggest either a new word or a revised interpretation of a term that has been included, please convey your recommendation to **dictionary99@hotmail.com**. The authors welcome your participation in helping to make the next edition even more comprehensive. They also invite you to contact them directly.

A

"A" Class Division

Bulkhead or deck that meets the following standard: constructed of steel or equivalent; capable of preventing the passage of smoke or flame; insulated so that the unexposed side will rise no more than 139 degrees centigrade from its original temperature within specified time periods, e.g. Class A-60, sixty minutes. For a more complete description, see **SOLAS** regulations.

Abandon Ship Drill

See **Lifeboat Drill**.

Abandonment

A ship's status when, due to severe damage, the vessel has been abandoned to the insurance underwriters as a constructive total loss, or abandoned to creditors. Compensation will be according to the insured amount, not the market value of the ship.

Abatement

Discount on an invoice occasioned by initial overcharge or damage to goods received.

ABC Islands

Acronym for Aruba, Bonaire, and Curaçao in the Netherlands Antilles.

Abeam

A nautical term meaning abreast, or to one side of a ship. Refers not to a point on the ship itself, but rather to one some distance away.

Able-Bodied Seamen (AB)

A crew member of the deck department, certified as such and with a number of years of experience. Experience requirements vary amongst cruise lines. See also **Deck** and **Engine**.

ABS

See **American Bureau of Shipping**.

Accommodation Ladder

Used to allow passengers or crew to board a

vessel. Accommodation ladders are connected to the side of a ship and, when deployed, sometimes require the user to climb a steep set of stairs before entering the ship. When not in use, accommodation ladders are stowed at deck level in a position horizontal to the sea. Such ladders are useful in ports where a ship can get **alongside** but where there are no well-developed terminal facilities that provide airline-style **gangways**. Usually a feature of older ships, modern cruise vessels have entrances through the side of the ship on lower decks that eliminate the need to climb steep stairs.

Accommodation Spaces

Defined by **SOLAS** to include public spaces, corridors, lavatories, cabins, offices, hospitals, cinemas, games and hobbies rooms, barber shops, pantries containing no cooking appliances, and similar spaces.

ACEPSOCSMM

See **American College of Emergency Physicians Section on Cruise Ship Maritime Medicine**.

Add-On

A supplementary charge that is added onto the price of the cruise. Most frequently applied to extra charges for air transportation to and from the ship when this is not included in the basic price of the cruise. The term is also used for such items as optional travel insurance, **pre - and post-cruise** hotel packages, **port charges,** air transportation upgrades, and other items for which there is additional cost on top of the basic fare. When dealing with air transportation, there may even be add-ons where air transportation is free – in cases where the passenger desires an upgrade to first or business class, or to deviate from the itinerary offered. See also **Deviation Desk**.

Addendum

A written comment made by a **classification society** inspector about a change or repair subsequent to the vessel's original classification.

Adjacent Zone

See **Contiguous Zone**.

Administration
   The **country of registry** that administers the affairs of a vessel. Normally, this expression is used in connection with international maritime law and regulations arising from it. References are made, for example, to The Bahamas as the administrator for all vessels under the Bahamian flag.

Admiralty Law
   The domestic and international laws that relate to maritime trade and marine operations including the transportation by sea of persons and property, harbors, ships and seamen. The word "admiralty" comes from the Arabic "amir" meaning commander, which is always followed by "al" (of the) and another word such as "ma" (water) or "bahr" (sea). The prefix "ad" was added and occurs in English beginning in 1205. See also **Maritime Law**.

Advance Notice of Arrival Requirements
   Effective January 26, 1998, the following **International Safety Management Code (ISM)** information is required of vessels prior to arrival in ports throughout the world: (1.) The date the **Document of Compliance (DOC)** was issued; (2.) The **Flag Administration** (or authorized organization) issuing the **DOC**; (3.) Date of issuance of the **Safety Management Certificate (SMC)**; (4.) The **Flag Administration** (or authorized organization) issuing the **SMC**.

Advance Ticket Sales Revenue
   See **Unearned Passenger Revenue**.

Adventure Cruise
   A category of cruise stressing primitive destinations such as Antarctica, the jungles of Central America, or the islands of the Galapagos; also, cruises to Alaska employing small ships and offering direct shore landings in undeveloped areas. Frequently, adventure cruises involve going ashore via rubber rafts (such as **zodiacs**), requiring passengers to don wading gear. Operations close inshore where there are no developed ports and, at times, no harbors most often require the use of small ships and, at times, those with hulls reinforced for navigation in ice. Best known of these are Abercrombie & Kent's *Explorer* (originally *Lindblad Explorer* and the first of

the breed); Society Expedition's *World Discoverer;* and Radisson Seven Seas' *Hanseatic.* However, larger vessels with reinforced hulls, such as Orient Line's 20,502 gross ton *Marco Polo,* can be used, provided the number of passengers does not exceed limitations imposed by environmental regulations, and that the crew can handle the number of passengers accommodated during the complicated and sometimes difficult shore transfers.

Aft

Toward the rear, back, or **stern** of a ship. The word is used more by ship's personnel than by the general public. When describing an event that is to take place in a public room aft, ship's staff will often use such expressions as "back of the ship", "rear of the ship" or even "stern of the ship," but rarely "aft". Traditionally, aft is a direction and stern, a location.

Afterbody

That portion of the **hull** aft of **amidships.**

Air Credit

Credit given to passengers participating in a cruise where airfare is normally included, but who wish to arrange their own transportation to the ship.

Air Draft

The maximum height of a ship above the **waterline.** This factor becomes an important consideration in planning cruise itineraries for individual vessels. Bridges at Philadelphia, Lisbon, Tampa, and other destinations prevent some ships from using these ports. This is also a factor when a **cruise ship** dock is near an airport.

Air & Sea Mix

The percentage of passengers aboard a **cruise ship** purchasing air transportation through the cruise line. This figure varies greatly according to itinerary and port where the ship is based. For instance, in cruises from San Juan, Puerto Rico, almost all passengers participate in **air/sea** programs. On Bermuda cruises from New York, a high percentage of passengers is drawn from the Middle Atlantic area and make their own way to the ship.

Airline Reporting Corporation (ARC)

Air Tour Operators License (ATOL)
Required by **Civil Aviation Authority (CAA)** for UK tour operators using charter flights. The ATOL is needed to satisfy CAA financial requirements for tour organizers.

Air/Sea (Program, Department, etc.)
A description of a package that includes airfare as well as the cruise portion of a trip. Transportation between the airport and the **cruise ship** is generally included as well. Often, there is a **meet and greet** service to escort passengers from the plane to the luggage area and on to surface transportation. Air/Sea is also frequently the name of the department within a cruise line that handles air arrangements. This department contracts with airlines and also with transfer companies. Responsibilities of this department vary from company to company, but may also include such items as air transportation for crew and executives of the line. The development of air/sea programs in the 1960's and 1970's made the modern cruise industry possible. For the first time, the airplane was the ally and not the enemy of ship transportation. These programs made possible the development of ports such as Miami, Port Everglades and San Juan, eliminating the need for passengers to endure two days of North Atlantic weather while en route to initial cruise destinations. A major event in the evolution of modern air/sea programs was the construction of the 10,563-ton *Golden Odyssey* of Royal Cruise Line in 1974. The vessel's initial capacity, 435, coincided with a Boeing 747 at full capacity. The ship's Mediterranean cruises could be filled by one round-trip charter.

Airline Reporting Corporation (ARC)
ARC is an international financial clearing house for the issuance of airline tickets. Many cruise lines have an in-house travel agency for handling **air/sea** reservations. As with travel agencies everywhere, ticket stock

Dictionary of the Cruise Industry

is issued by ARC and payment made to the corporation. Entities using ARC must post a bond with the corporation to guarantee payment for tickets that are issued by the agency or cruise line.

Alleyway

A narrow passageway. On a vessel the reference is normally to corridors on passenger or officer/crew cabin decks. This is traditional maritime parlance and not used frequently at the present time.

Allotment (Allocation)

(1) Block of cabins reserved in advance for a single sailing or series of cruises for a tour operator or group organizer; (2) percentage of a seaman's wages which is automatically paid to a designee in the seaman's home country.

Alongside

Describes the position of a vessel that is docked at a pier, in contrast with those situations when a vessel is at anchor. In the latter case, a ship must embark or disembark passengers via **tender.** The **draft** of modern **cruise ships,** frequently twenty-five feet or less, plus the continuing development of **ports** means it is likely that a ship will be able to go alongside in many, perhaps the majority, of ports.

Alternating Itineraries

Itineraries in which a ship alternates two fixed routes. The most common alternating itineraries are those from South Florida to the Eastern or Western Caribbean. Other examples, usually involving longer cruises, are from a British, Dutch or German port to the Norwegian fjords or the Baltic; and from an Italian or Greek port to the Eastern or Western Mediterranean. Among the advantages of alternating itineraries are the ability of passengers to remain aboard a ship for two successive cruises to different destinations; attraction of repeat passengers to the same ship on a different itinerary; and the ability to offer two products with one ship. Also known as a **"butterfly" itinerary** because the route, represented on a map, is often roughly in the shape of a butterfly.

Alternative Dining

Dining apart from the ship's main dining room, especially at dinner. The term usually refers to the option of having dinner in a smaller, themed setting – either in a room created just for this purpose, or in the ship's casual restaurant with more formal settings and with decor augmented for the evening. In most cases, reservations are required and there may or may not be an extra charge to cover gratuities. Another example of alternative dining is aboard the "Grand Class" ships of Princess Cruises where sit-down dining is available on a twenty-four hour basis in a location apart from the ship's main dining room. A variation on the alternative dining concept is the Disney pattern of moving passengers, together with their servers, to different dining rooms on successive nights to provide greater variety in the dining experience.

American Bureau of Shipping (ABS)

The American **classification society** that, like its overseas counterparts, certifies compliance with **IMO** standards relating to construction, design, and maintenance of ships. Certification that a vessel meets **SOLAS** and other **IMO** standards is in the hands of the **country of registry**. The U.S.'s chosen instrument for exercising this responsibility for American ships is the ABS.

American College of Emergency Physicians Section on Cruise Ship Maritime Medicine (ACEPSOCMM)

Representing over three hundred physicians, all of them U.S.-registered, the organization has the avowed purpose of encouraging partnerships among **cruise ship** companies, passengers, and medical staff. It maintains a job bank. In 1995, ACEPSOCMM published the world's first set of detailed operational guidelines for medical facilities on board ship.

Amidships

Nautical term for the middle section of the ship.

Anchor

Device that connects a ship's mooring chain to the

Anchorage

ocean or harbor bottom. Has prongs that tend to dig into the harbor bottom and prevent "dragging" (where the anchor does not hold and therefore does not maintain the ship in a stationary position). Most often, **cruise ships** are equipped with two anchors. Mounted on each side of the bow, anchors in this position have traditionally been called "bower" anchors. Special operating conditions may prompt a third or fourth anchor to be mounted in the bow and/or one in the stern. The latter is useful where vessels must occasionally anchor in a river with the bow pointing in a downstream direction. The stern anchor is a common feature of ships regularly sailing the St. Lawrence River to Quebec City and/or Montreal, Canada.

Anchorage

Location where a ship may anchor. This is usually within a harbor, but may also be off-shore in an unprotected location. In the cruise industry, anchorages must frequently be used when docks are unavailable or too small. Examples are the Mexican port of Playa del Carmen, and St. John in the U.S. Virgin Islands. The term can be incorrectly used in a situation where the water is too deep to anchor and a ship essentially drifts, held in position through engines and **bow thrusters**. An example of such a port is the Greek island of Santorini. Good **holding ground**, where the seabed is such that an anchor will take hold rather than drag and keep the ship in position, is, of course, desirable.

Anti-heeling System

Allows for quick recovery from a **list**. Consists of a series of small ballast tanks low in the **hull**. Functions through a computerized monitoring and control system. This system supplements the ship's major system for control of stability that consists of very large tanks deep in the **hull**.

Antifouling Paint

Paint generally used below the waterline that, through its chemical composition, inhibits marine growth. Due to advances in antifouling paint, it is now desirable to put a ship in dry dock only every other year and essential only twice in five years. In earlier days, this expensive process was necessary each year and was often done more often.

API (Administracion Portuaria Integral)
The unit of port administration in Mexico. The country has a decentralized system of port administration, and has privatized some port operations. With over ten cruise ports bordering the Gulf, the Caribbean and the Pacific, Mexico has the most cruise passenger arrivals among the world's port countries.

Approved
In **SOLAS,** approved by the country of **administration.** This underscores the responsibility of the country where a ship is registered for enforcement of regulations promulgated by the **International Maritime Organization (IMO)**, including those in **SOLAS.**

Area of Dominant Influence (ADI)
The area where a group of radio or TV stations, or newspapers, have a dominant influence. This is an alternate term for "media market."

Area Sales Manager
See **District Sales Manager.**

Arrest
When a vessel has been taken into the custody of the court because a creditor asserts a **maritime lien** has been placed on a vessel. In port, local authorities have the right to arrest a ship, not allowing it to load or unload passengers, crew, or cargo, or to leave port until the lien has been lifted. The term **seizure** is sometimes used at times when referring to arrest. A major example in recent times was the arrest of *Regent Rainbow* in Tampa, Florida for non-payment of a caterer's bill. The act led to the bankruptcy and demise of Regency Cruises and the arrest of its ships in several ports.

Arrival Notification
Required advance notice of arrival for a given port. If a **berth** is required, a reservation up to two years in advance may be needed. See **Advance Notice of Arrival Requirements.**

Art Auction
The sale of art aboard ship. These auctions have

become an established part of the on board program aboard many ships.

Astern

Toward or beyond the back of a vessel. When a ship reverses or backs, it is said to go astern.

Athens Convention Relating to the Carriage of Passengers and Their Luggage by Sea (1974)

Applies to the carriage of passengers and their luggage by sea and limits cruise line liability. Except for non-ratification by the United States, the 1974 Convention is an international treaty. Currently, the Convention limits liability payments to $46,666 per person "special joint rights" or approximately $70,000 under current exchange rates (at time of writing, under review). For ships operating outside U.S. jurisdiction, the Athens Convention provides a framework for dealing with lawsuits relating to plaintiff's cruise and the passenger contract governing it. See also **Passenger Contract**.

Athwartships

Directional term meaning across a ship, perpendicular to the length of the vessel.

ATOL

See **Air Tour Operators License**.

Available Berths

The term denotes the total number of passenger days a ship can offer for sale in any given year. It is used as a reference point for projections of revenue on a per person basis. Potential annual occupancy is not automatically the number of **lower berths** x 365. This number will vary from one year to another under the following circumstances: a vessel is in dry or wet dock, taking the ship out of service for a certain period; a ship is undergoing cabin renovation and the rooms being renovated are taken out of the inventory of cabins that can be sold even though the ship remains in service; or passenger cabins are used for staff, e.g. entertainment staff.

Average Cruise Length

One way of profiling the operations of a cruise line, of a market, or of the entire industry. In 1995, the Average Cruise Length of the industry was 6.5 days. Although many **cruise ships** offer longer voyages such as **Transcanal Cruises** and many in European waters, the average length of the cruises is heavily influenced by the large number of vessels with substantial capacities that operate out of South Florida and in the Greek Islands, among other places, on two-, three- and four-day cruises.

Azipods (Brand Name)
See **Podded Azimuthing Propulsors**.

B

"B" Class Division
A bulkhead, deck, ceiling, lining or deck constructed of **noncombustible material** that prevents the passage of flame for a half hour under standard fire test conditions, and that meets other standards set forth in **SOLAS** regulations.

Back-to-Back
Most often, two consecutive cruises taken by a passenger on the same ship from the same home port. The term is also occasionally used to denote a passenger taking two segments of a longer cruise where the sailings are sold primarily as separate cruises.

BAF
See **Bunker Adjustment Factor**.

Baggage Policy
The amount of baggage that may be brought on a cruise varies from line to line and may or may not be listed in company brochures. Liability is fixed by the **Athens Convention**. Frequently, lines depend on the air carrier to limit passenger baggage through excess baggage charges and other policies.

Balcony Cabin (Veranda Cabin)
An outside cabin with a balcony. Current building practice is to include as many of these as the vessel's **superstructure** and, sometimes, the **hull** can accommodate – as many as 23 - 55% of all cabins. In past years, balconies were limited to

ultra deluxe sections of the vessel (the pre-war *Normandie* of the French Line had several suites with balconies and Italian Line's pre-war *Saturnia* and *Vulcania* extended this amenity to a number of first class outside cabins). The *Royal Princess* introduced the practice of providing balconies for a large number of otherwise standard outside rooms. The vessel, introduced in 1984, offers 21% of her cabins with balconies. Silversea, in the ultra-deluxe segment of the cruise market, provides a balcony for each cabin. In the mainstream of mass market cruising, *Carnival Destiny*, introduced in the fall of 1996, offers 432 or 32.7% of its rooms with balcony. One of the highest balcony percentages is aboard *Grand Princess* where 55% of cabins have verandas. The reason for this trend? The magic of balcony cabins in the marketplace and the willingness of passengers to pay extra for them. Verandas give to rooms not only outdoor space but offer far more glass area than other types of cabins. With the door open and a breeze circulating throughout the room, the entire cabin seems like a balcony.

Ballast

Weight carried by a vessel to maintain or improve stability. Most frequently, this takes the form of tanks containing liquid – seawater, fuel, etc. If a miscalculation has occurred in the design of a vessel – which was the case with P & O's *Canberra*, *Leonardo da Vinci*, and the 1912 German liner *Imperator*, permanent solid ballast may have to be placed low in the ship in order to maintain the safety or **trim** of the vessel. This increases drag and decreases the earning capacity of a ship. On a **cruise ship,** stability is maintained through pumps that regulate the location of water, fuel, and other liquid ballast. A ship may also take on additional ballast, or dispose of it in keeping with applicable environmental regulations. The ability to transfer ballast is also useful in keeping a ship upright in the event of damage and flooding. It is, for instance, a basic element of warship damage control.

Bare Boat Charter

A charter of a **cruise ship** from an owner to an

operator whereby the charterer assumes all responsibility for operating the vessel including staffing, insurance, and marine operation. Also referred to as "bareboat charter," "demise charter," or a "demise."

Barecon

A standard contract, also referred to as the **Norwegian Form**, that has been adopted by the Baltic and International Maritime Conference to be used world wide for **bare boat charters** of all types of vessels. The agreement allows for insertion of all the important information about the charter and its conditions.

Barratry

An illegal act by the master or crew of a vessel for which owners are liable. This term is used where the act is done without the knowledge of the owners. An example: dumping oil-polluted water into the ocean against company policy and international regulations, creating legal exposure for the cruise line. Historically, barratry was equated with piracy and referred to fraud or theft committed by the Master and/or his officers.

Basis Point

Pro-mil (0.01%). A unit of percentage often discussed in negotiations involving interest rates and loans.

Beam

The extreme width of a ship at its widest part. Most vessels are restricted by the **Panamax Standard** governing length and beam. Panamax vessels are the largest ships capable of transiting the Panama Canal. In 1996, Carnival Cruise Lines introduced the *Carnival Destiny*, the first purpose-built **cruise ship** with a beam wider than the Panamax standard, referred to as "Post-Panamax size." While beam is both a traditional and comprehensive term, the synonym breadth has also come into use by **SOLAS**, and with reference to drydocking. "Beam at pool decks," increased by **sponsons** extending out from the superstructure, can be a substantially different from hull beam and becomes a factor in traversing canals and other narrow waterways, such as the Corinth Canal.

Bear, or Bearing

Refers to the direction of another ship or object in reference to the observer aboard a vessel at sea, or the direction relative to the bow ("Bearing thirty degrees on the starboard bow"). The bearing is expressed in terms of a compass direction (north, south, etc.), degree, or both. Abbreviations: Bring or Bg.

Bearing

See **Bear**.

Beaufort Scale

The Beaufort Scale is the official scale that describes wind force and sea conditions on a scale from one to twelve. The Beaufort Scale was devised by a British Admiral, Sir Francis Beaufort, in the mid-nineteenth century. This scale is widely used by officers to describe the condition of the sea. On every bridge of every ship, a description of the Beaufort Scale is posted, including criteria for sea height and wind strength for each force on the scale, illustrated by photographs. Aboard **cruise ships,** this scale is frequently used to advise passengers of sea conditions in addition to its use as the official measure for purposes of **log** notations.

Bell

A compulsory piece of equipment installed on the bow where it can best be heard. The bell is used in conditions of restricted visibility. It is sounded when the anchor is dropped or pulled up, advising ships in the area about the vessel's intentions and activity. In the modern cruise industry, in an era of satellite navigation and radar, its importance has declined.

Bell, Gongs, and Whistle Certificate

Certificate issued by a ship's **classification society** or **administration** indicating that the vessel complies with **IMO** regulations regarding bells, gongs, and whistles.

Berth

(1) A bed, generally attached to the **deck** and/or

bulkhead, on board a ship; (2) an anchorage or dock space for a ship in port.

Berth Allocation

(1) An industry term, used by **Cruise Lines International Association (CLIA),** travel media, and analysts to describe the number of **berths** allocated to specific **cruise areas** by one or more cruise lines; or (2) the allocation of spaces in a **port** to a cruise line or ship.

Berth Days

Number of lower **berths** times days of operation.

Berth Trials

Tests of machinery, electrical, and piping systems while the ship is stationary in its **berth** at the shipyard. In ships of Carnival Corporation, for example, this involves operating the main propulsion unit at the maximum practical speed for at least six hours. The purpose is to detect defects while there is still time to correct them prior to delivery of the vessel, and to prove readiness for sea trials. See also **yard trials** and **sea trials**.

Berthing Book

These have almost disappeared from the passenger reservation scene. Prior to the computer era, passenger reservations were made in a series of books bearing a ship's cabin numbers in which passenger information was written by hand as reservations were made. The name of the booking agent was also included. Reservation agents had large revolving carousels with a book for each sailing. When the computer era arrived, veteran reservation agents would not let go of their beloved berthing books and continued for a time to make parallel reservations – one in the book and another in electronic format. After full computerization was completed, some lines organized a "burning of the berthing books" party. The berthing book has also been used by **harbor masters** to plan berthing assignments for ships using the port.

Bibby Cabin

See **L-Shaped Cabin (Bibby Cabin).**

Bilge

The bottom of a ship on either side of the **keel**.

This is where water that seeps into a ship tends to collect, thus the need for bilge pumps. It is also the location of **ballast** tanks used to store sea water or fuel, the manipulation of which helps keep the ship on an even keel free of **list** and with the correct degree of stability.

Bill of Sale

A deed that assigns personal property from one entity to another. In the shipping and cruise industry, the bill of sale of a registered ship includes information such as the ship's registry number, a description of it, and includes all conditions of the transaction. A bill of sale is governed by various merchant shipping acts in different countries, but all are based on the original **British Merchant Marine Act** which specifies the information that must be included and regulates other issues concerning a sale.

Binnacle

Non-magnetic stand that houses a ship's compass.

Black Squall

A storm or weather front, frequently found in the tropics, where the clouds are dark announcing an imminent and pronounced deterioration in weather conditions.

Block Booking (Drydocking Facilities)

Made by a cruise line to arrange for the drydocking of several ships in a fleet consecutively. This yields increased bargaining power and priority in obtaining the services of a shipyard during peak periods. Overhauls are generally undertaken by all cruise lines during slack booking times, notably the fall. Priority in accomplishing this work in the shipyard of choice can be a major financial and operational issue. The price, workmanship, and distance a ship must travel away from its terminal port are all factors.

Block Coefficient

The extent to which the underwater portion of a vessel fully occupies the water within a rectangular block representing underwater length, width, and draft. The block coefficient indicates whether the lines of a ship are concave and streamlined (as with a fast ship) or convex and portly. The underwater portion of a fast Atlantic liner may have occupied little more than half of this dimension. The corresponding hull sector of a modern **cruise ship** would occupy much more than this.

Blue Card
A membership card for the **International Transport Workers Federation (ITF)**.

BNM
See **Broadcast Notice to Mariners**.

Boarding Pass
Issued at time of check-in, this enables passengers not only to board the ship initially but, most often, to reboard the vessel throughout the cruise. Often, this takes the form of a plastic card that is also used for shipboard charge accounts.

Cruise ships are now high-security areas, and the form of passenger identification is of high importance.

BOB
See **Booking on Board**.

Bollard
A vertical projection from the pier or from the **deck** of a ship, made of steel or wood, to which a docked ship is tied or that secures the ship's end of a **mooring line**. The **line man** attaches a ship's mooring rope to the bollard on the pier where the ship is docking, and removes it on departure whereupon the mooring line is hauled on board the ship.

Bond Port
See **Port of Entry**.

Bonded Warehouse
Conveniently located for shipping and access from cruise ports, these are used for storing merchandise and other materials such as spare parts that have entered the country but on which no customs duty has been paid. Items can be re-exported, but not sold in the country where stored. The bond is posted with customs to ensure that local sale does not occur. Such bonding is an international practice. See also **In Bond**.

Booking Form
In the UK, a reservation form that must be completed at time of booking, one per cabin, by legal requirement. The form solicits such information as the following: special dietary requirements; insurance provided or available; air and hotel options; disabilities, if any; and dining room seating preferences. Another such form is used in other countries of the European Union.

Booking on Board (BOB)
Reservation for a future cruise made by passengers on board ship.

Boot Top
A broad stripe, used on some vessels to provide contrasting color at the waterline. On a passenger ship, the bottom edge is invariably beneath the surface of the water. Not to be confused with the thin white or gold stripe used at the waterline as ornamentation on some ships. The term had more significance in the days when all ships carried some cargo. The boot top covered the area between the waterline when the ship was fully loaded, and the waterline when the vessel was empty. Most **cruise ships** now have all the underwater part of the ship painted the same color. On a **cruise ship**, some of this is always visible above the waterline. The visible portion is still referred to as the boot top. Often, a special paint mixture is used to withstand repeated wetting and drying.

Booze Cruises
Term sometimes used for "cruises to nowhere" taken for purposes of gambling, partying, etc. The term is not used at the present time, in marked contrast to the days of prohibition in the United States where in a typical week thousands of passengers sailed from New York on four- and five day cruises to Bermuda, Nassau, or Canada/New England to escape the prohibition against liquor sale, manufacture, and consumption. In the days of several weekly transatlantic services prior to World War II, ships usually had to remain idle in New York for several days for companies to maintain regular weekly Atlantic services. For those with medium-speed ships, three vessels were too many

and two, not enough. Thus, "booze cruises" were an attractive way of reducing losses in an era when transatlantic travel was plummeting. It is probably not coincidental that the parade of older Atlantic liners to the shipbreakers did not begin in earnest until the repeal of the Volstead Act and prohibition in 1933. There is frequent current usage of the term with reference to trips on excursion boats in ports of call that feature an open bar.

Bos'un (Boatswain)
The foreman who is responsible for supervising all deck department responsibilities. He generally reports directly to the chief officer, staff captain, or to the captain.

Bottom Scraping
Eliminates marine growth from a ship's bottom during **drydocking**. These cause **drag**, and can slow a ship as well as increase fuel costs. Formerly necessary once each year, most cruise lines now find this desirable every two years though it is required just twice in five. This is due to advances in the development of marine anti-fouling paint. Further development is in process that will increase still further the intervals between drydockings.

Bouillon at 11 A.M.
A tradition of serving clear soup on deck dating from transatlantic steamship service where temperatures were brisk. The same ships continued to offer this when they cruised, and it has been adopted as a late-morning beverage break by many cruise lines.

Boutique Ship
A small but very luxurious all-suite **cruise ship**. Examples: the ships of Silversea and Windstar. The first such ships were *Sea Goddess I* and *Sea Goddess II* originally of Sea Goddess Cruises but later part of the Cunard Fleet (now Cunard Seabourn). The Sea Goddess ships are of 4,620 tons carrying a maximum of 116 passengers in all-deluxe accommodation. This category of ship has been more notable for high standards of accommodation than for profitability. Interestingly, they are the same size as the first dedicated **cruise ships** at the turn of the Nineteenth/Twentieth Centuries but, of course, offer much more luxurious spaces for passengers.

Bow
Front of a ship's hull.

Bow Thruster
Propeller(s) installed in a tunnel extending across the ship under the water line. When activated, the thruster swings the ship sideways. Formerly found just in the bow, most modern **cruise ships** also feature them in the stern. However, stern thrusters are not necessary in ships with azimuthing podded propulsion systems. These eliminate the need for tugboats under most conditions, greatly aiding the maneuvering of a ship in confined waters or when docking. The 1959 express British Liner *Oriana* set the modern pattern with two bow and two stern thrusters. The new **megaships** have increasing numbers of these to deal adequately with the effect of wind on these high-sided vessels when maneuvering.

Branding/Brand Management
The creation of different cruise lines representing varying cruise products by a single corporation. This is done to attract additional cruise passengers of different nationality, demographics, or vacation taste than are attracted to the initial product. Additional brands may be created by purchase or by new product creation. Two examples are Royal Caribbean International's acquisition of Celebrity Cruises; and Carnival Corporation's acquisition of Holland America/Windstar, Costa, Seabourn, Airtours and Cunard for a total of seven Carnival Corporation brands.

Breadth
See **Beam.**

Breakbulk
Non-containerized cargo. Until the advent of year-round **cruise ships,** passenger vessels frequently carried high-grade breakbulk cargo, sometimes in large quantities. The dawn of the container age doomed some long-distance passenger services that depended heavily on cargo revenue, notably those of Union Castle Line and some of Shaw Savill, when it became advantageous to haul cargo in a different type of vessel.

Bridge

The area from which the ship's officers navigate a vessel. On a **cruise ship**, the bridge is generally found high up and forward and is the location of steering controls and a variety of computerized navigational devices. Most modern bridges, including the **bridge wings,** are completely enclosed by glass and climate-controlled.

Bridge Wings

Projections from the superstructure of a ship abreast the navigating bridge. Until the 1990's, most bridge wings were open to the sky. In new ships, they are enclosed and air-conditioned so that it is possible to place computerized equipment, such as **joysticks,** in these vantage points without having them and the officers exposed to the elements and high humidity.

Brig

Traditional name for a jail or detention area aboard ship.

Broadcast Notice to Mariners (BNM)

Broadcast notice to mariners – radio transmissions warning of potential marine hazards, including: hurricanes, oil spills, dredging, etc.

Budget Cruises

Cruises priced below those in the mass market. These tend to be aboard smaller, older ships lacking in megaship amenities but popular with shiplovers. Many are former ocean **liners** that have a unique charm. Due to the massive economies of scale that megaships deliver, there is very little space in the marketplace for cruises priced below the mass market giants. A few lines in this category still operate: Regal Cruises, Premier Cruise Lines, and Commodore Cruise Line.

Builder's Certificate

A certificate issued by the shipyard attesting that the vessel is in compliance with the specifications under which she was ordered.

Building Certificate

Produced by the shipyard for the owner on **delivery** of a vessel, it includes general information on the ship. Detailed information on machinery,

stability, speed and other major areas is contained in operator manuals.

Bulbous Bow

Bulb-shaped construct beneath the **waterline** at a ship's bow. Also known as the "bulb", this reduces the size of the bow wave and resistance as a ship moves through the water. The bulbous bow was introduced to passenger ship design by the NDL liners *Bremen* and *Europa* in 1929 and 1930. They quickly garnered the Atlantic speed record for passenger ships. Design of the bulbous bow has become much more sophisticated since then and is a feature of almost all new passenger ships. Properly designed, it reduces fuel consumption by three to six percent.

Bulkhead

A wall on a ship. Sometimes bulkheads are watertight or fireproof, becoming part of the ship's safety system; in other places, they are merely like walls in a home and divide spaces for functional rather than safety reasons.

Bulkhead Deck

The highest deck up to which watertight bulkheads extend.

Bunker Adjustment Factor (BAF)

Sometimes referred to as Fuel Adjustment Factor, it is an adjustment of fares or charter rates to compensate a shipowner for fluctuation in the price of fuel. This becomes a commonly used term in periods of wild fluctuations in the cost of oil, such as during the Arab Oil Embargo in the early 1970's when the cost of a ton of bunker fuel went from $20 to over $100.

Bunker Station

Aboard ship, the location of connections for fueling the vessel. They are located just inside the **hull**, and accessible from the outside via a door.

Bunkers

Marine fuel used for propulsion. Bunkers are traditionally fuel storage spaces, but in this century the meaning of this term has evolved to include not only the spaces but the contents of them. As a place for storing fuel, it was more often used when coal was the primary source of energy for propulsion. Now, the term "fuel tank" most often denotes the fuel storage space.

Burdened Vessel

The vessel required to **"give way"** in a passing or crossing situation. Also known as the "give way" vessel.

Bus Program

Where bus transportation is provided to and from the ship at the port of departure and port of return. This is often a feature of cruises from New York and other Middle Atlantic ports, and is also used for many cruises from Port Canaveral and South Florida. In Europe, this mode of transfer is frequently used in Venice, Genoa, Amsterdam, and Copenhagen.

Butterfly Itinerary

An **alternating itinerary**. When represented on a map, an alternating itinerary frequently has the shape of a butterfly. Good examples of this are alternating itineraries in the Eastern and Western Caribbean as well as Eastern and Western Mediterranean.

C

"C" Class Division

Constructed of approved non-combustible materials, these do not have to meet the standards included in "A" or "B" divisions. Until 2005, this standard permits the use of combustible veneers that meet the requirements of **SOLAS** regulations. The SOLAS text and amendments should be consulted for further details on this and other class divisions.

CAA

See **Civil Aviation Authority.**

Cabin

A room that accommodates passengers or crew on board a vessel. In modern ships, cabins have achieved the standardization associated with hotels. In older vessels with more curvaceous **hull** lines, there were commonly as many as twenty or thirty cabin configurations and sizes, each with its own fare level. The most important cabin categories aboard a modern ship are **inside cabin, outside cabin, balcony cabin,** single cabin, and **suite.** Unless otherwise stated, a cabin is presumed to have two lower beds. There may be one or more upper berths. A **family cabin,** available on a few new **cruise ships** such as Celebrity's *Galaxy, Mercury,* and the Disney ships, accommodates four or five people with greater space and comfort than is possible with four in a standard cabin. These sometimes have a sleeping area for children separated by movable panels from the adult beds. Cabin categories and definition will vary from one cruise line and ship class to another. The term **stateroom** is a traditional word used to connote a spacious, well-fitted cabin or cabin deluxe.

Cabin Configuration

The interior layout of a cabin. Most common variations: twin-bed, upper and lower, standard, deluxe, suite, family cabin (accommodating four or more), type of bathroom facility (shower or tub bath), and occasionally, type of window. In the days before most cabins were rectangular and prefabricated, designers provided "L-Shaped" or "Bibby" cabins that enabled otherwise inside cabins to have access to a **porthole** through a narrow corridor to the side of the ship. This is inconsistent with modern construction methods and, in these days of complete air conditioning, less necessary than it once was.

Cabin Mock-Up

Full-sized model of a cabin, usually a standard cabin. This is done when preparing a new ship design, whether for one vessel or for an entire class. The mock-up is then used by architects to perfect the design to maximize comfort, appearance, ease of maintenance, and to facilitate the final selection of materials, hardware, and finishes. Once a design is complete, the mock-up is used as a reference for contractors and is photographed for preliminary brochures.

Cabotage

The word cabotage comes from the French word "caboter" which means to sail "by the capes". In the cruise industry, cabotage laws relate to the ability of foreign-flag vessels to transport passengers between domestic ports. Most countries of the world have some cabotage laws to protect ships registered under their own flags and to prevent foreign carriers from competing with the country's own flag companies. Cabotage laws are also, at times, known as **coastwise shipping laws**. Examples of strong cabotage regulations are those in Greece where the Greek cruise lines have the exclusive right to carry passengers between Greek islands until 1999. The United States also has a series of cabotage laws commonly and erroneously known as the **Jones Act**. Actually, the Jones Act relates to the carriage of cargo and seamen's rights; it is the **Passenger Services Act (PSA)** that restricts the transport of passengers between U.S. ports on foreign-flag vessels. Coastwise laws have been slightly relaxed to accommodate cruise operations and are a perennial subject of controversy.

Cage

Steel container used to collect passenger luggage prior to embarkation for transfer to the vessel; and prior to disembarkation, for transfer to the pier where luggage is collected by passengers. During the voyage, the containers fold to save space. Cages are five feet tall and the size of pallets. Now used by many lines, the concept was originated by Meshulam Zonis, Senior Vice President for Operations, Carnival Cruise Lines. The term is also used universally – aboard ship and ashore – for the location in a casino where a cashier undertakes casino-related cash transactions.

California Cruise Ship Revitalization Act

An amendment to the Johnson Act, which allows states to regulate gambling outside state waters if the voyage begins and ends in the same state, and the ship does visit any other state or nation within three days (or 72 hours). This amendment, passed by the US Congress in September, 1996, overturned the gambling ban imposed on the cruise industry by the California Attorney General in 1993. The ban prevented **cruise ships** calling at more than one California port on international voyages from opening casinos at sea. The ban hurt California ports and, in the case of San Diego, reduced the number of calls from 500 in 1991 to close to zero in 1995. A coalition of interested parties from San Diego and other cities lobbied Congress to pass the Revitalization Act. The measure has been effective in that vessels have resumed their calls at San Diego.

Call Sign

Each registered vessel has a call sign, usually a combination of letters and numbers, that is the Communication ID of the vessel when using the radio on the high seas. The call sign remains even when the vessel changes ownership (though not when there is a change of registry). This used to be part of the information provided to passengers in preparation for a cruise so that friends and relatives could contact them if necessary. Now, telephone numbers suffice.

Callable Loan

A loan that can be collected at the discretion of the lender, subject to any restrictions that are in the loan covenant or agreement. This is a "weak" loan that gives the lender the option of collecting money loaned before the cruise line or other enterprise enters bankruptcy.

Cancellation Policy

A policy that outlines the penalties paid by a passenger for cancelling a reservation. The policy is set forth to ensure that the line has sufficient time to resell a cancelled cabin. Obviously, the closer to the departure date, the higher the penalty. Many cruise lines offer trip cancellation insurance which allows passengers, upon payment of a premium, to make plans for a cruise, yet be able to abort the plans if necessary (for example, in the case of sudden illness). Each cruise line has its own cancellation policy which varies from line to line. For example, Princess Cruises has no cancellation penalty if a cruise is cancelled sixty days or more in advance. For 59 to 31 days, the penalty is the amount of the deposit. 30 -15 days: 50% of the total charge; 14 days - 72 hours: 75% of total charges; less than 72 hours: 100% of total charges.

Capacity, Passenger

In the cruise industry, the number of lower berths. Sometimes, the term "lower-berth capacity" is used. Many vessels have large numbers of cabins with three or four berths, useful for flexibility in booking families and friends travelling together. However, the total actual number of berths may exceed the dining room capacity and other limitations, so total number of beds (upper and lower) is sometimes not really a valid indicator of a ship's practical capacity. However, counting all passengers in all berths does explain the situation where a cruise line has averaged more than 100% of capacity during a given period.

Capacity Utilization

Occupancy rate of a fleet or of the total industry. In 1996, the industry capacity utilization was 88%, the highest ever. This figure usually includes reduced-rate and **comp** travelers as well as those cruising at normal fares.

Captain

See **Master**.

Captain's Cocktail Party

Usually occurs on the second or third day of the cruise; held so that passengers may meet the Captain and, most often, other officers and cruise staff. During such a reception, passengers are usually introduced to the Captain by the Hostess as they enter the lounge where the party is taking place. The Captain shakes hands with the passengers, and a photographer takes pictures. This is also an opportunity to introduce the ship's concession staff and to advertise such optional activities as hairdressing and massage. As ships grow in size, the Captain's Cocktail Party may well become a thing of the past. Captains on ships assigned to three- and four-day cruises have to shake hands with 2,600 passengers twice each week, facing camera flashes each time. At this point, the custom becomes impractical. On some vessels, duties are shared with one of the other senior officers. Occasionally, a captain may understandably be seen looking away from the camera in photos that are taken at these marathon sessions. This is in some contrast to the days of the Atlantic liners, many of them equal in size to **cruise ships** of today, but where first class passengers only were invited to this event.

Captain's Farewell Dinner

This dinner is usually served on the next-to-last night of the cruise on sailings of seven days or more. It is an opportunity for the Captain to dine with the passengers and is normally a formal event. In many cases, it is preceded by a cocktail party. In cases of multiple dining rooms/seatings, the Captain will dine only once but may put in an appearance in other dining rooms and seatings.

Captain's Table

Since the early days of ocean travel, the principal dining room on most ships has had a table designated as the Captain's Table. This table was used for the Captain to dine with other passengers. This tradition still exists in most cruise lines, although actual practices vary widely according to company customs and the individual preferences of captains. Frequently, the Captain's Table is the subject of company written policy specifying the category of invitations and the number of nights the Captain is expected to dine with passengers. The Captain normally invites to his table very important guests such as inspection VIP's, travel agents, travel press, large group organizers, company executives and other dignitaries who are cruising. Often, the courtesy will be extended to friends of the Captain. The vessel's hostess normally tenders invitations and accepts RSVP's. Modern **cruise ships** have comparatively elaborate dining facilities for the Captain and for his senior officers, many of whom prefer to dine with peers. Like many other maritime traditions, this is an endangered one as ships and passenger lists get larger and the captain's job pressures increase.

Captain's Welcome Dinner
This normally occurs the second night of the cruise. During this dinner, which the Captain attends, the Captain is introduced to the passengers. It is a formal night and in some cases, is preceded by the **Captain's Cocktail Party**. If there are two seatings or two dining rooms, the Captain makes sure to be seen in all seatings in all dining rooms and may speak to each group. Many **cruise ships** are equipped with a captain's table in each dining room.

Carferry
A vessel designed to carry cars and, generally, people. In the period since 1960, these have evolved into mini-**liners** and **cruise ships** with extensive and elaborate accommodation for passengers. For the role of the carferry in the development of the modern **cruise ship,** see **cruise ship**.

Caribbean Shore Excursion Liability (CASEL)
Through the intervention of the **Florida Caribbean Cruise Association (FCCA)**, the firm of Lombart, Fenchurch & Atlas provides affordable liability insurance accessible to small Caribbean excursion operators. This has had the effect of broadening the range of **shore excursions** that can be offered by a cruise line by placing liability insurance within the reach of operators that otherwise would be unable to afford coverage.

Carrier
A description of a cruise line for the purposes of regulations, federal laws, etc.; also applies to airlines.

CASEL
See **Caribbean Shore Excursion Liability**.

Cashless
Refers to system whereby cash is normally not accepted for purchases on board. Usually, all on-board expenses except for gratuities (and, with most companies, gambling expenses), are billed to the individual for payment on the final morning of the cruise via cash or automatic credit card billing. Passengers then receive an itemized billing before leaving the ship. This system offers greater

Cast Off

passenger convenience and far tighter auditing controls. Passengers are given a disposable temporary charge card good for all expenses. Actual credit cards and signatures are registered at the start of the cruise. The card may also serve as a room key and boarding pass. Thanks to a "smart card" concept being developed, possible future uses include studying the flow of passengers aboard ship, medical information, data on airline arrangements, and many other purposes.

Cast Off

To let go the **mooring lines**; to sail. The term is normally used when sailing from a pier.

Casual Dress

When used as a recommended form of dress for an evening aboard ship, generally means that men need not wear jacket or tie but may wear a sport shirt and slacks, and women may don comparable attire.

Casual Elegance

A marketing term that defies exact definition, used by some cruise lines such as Windstar, Club Med, or Princess to describe a style of cruising or dress for an evening. When used on board a ship to describe dress for a casual night, it is hoped that passengers will don expensive or dressy casual wear rather than worn jeans and other similar apparel.

Catamaran

A double-hulled vessel. In **cruise ship** design, catamaran configuration offers good resistance to rolling and shallow draft. However, the heavier structure required of these craft makes them more expensive than single-hulled ships of comparable size and capacity. The first and only major catamaran **cruise ship** is the *Radisson Diamond*.

Category

A group of cabins with similar characteristics, or equivalent characteristics, sold at the same fare. In the UK, the more common term is **grade**.

Cavitation

Turbulent flow of water on a **propeller** blade, **stabilizer**, **rudder**, or propeller bracket, creating vacuum pockets which collapse causing pressure pulses. A common remedy for propeller cavitation is replacement with those of a revised design. Propeller designs are commonly optimized by testing scale models in water tunnels. However, errors are still rather common in new designs considering the cost of the remedy.

Cay
See **Key**.

CDC
See **Centers for Disease Control (CDC)**.

Ceiling Pullman
An upper **pullman** bed that retracts into a ceiling recess, for the third or fourth passenger in a cabin. Ceiling pullmans have been installed in several new **cruise ships**. A standard pullman is hinged and folds up against the **bulkhead**.

Centers for Disease Control (CDC)
The Centers for Disease Control and Prevention is part of the U.S. Department of Health and Human Services and has instituted voluntary sanitation standards for vessels calling at U.S. ports. Publicly distributed reports, popularly called **Green Sheets**, are distributed free to anyone requesting a copy. More detailed information on any ship is also provided on request. CDC oversees the **Vessel Sanitation Program** and conducts two unannounced inspections per year of **cruise ships** calling at U.S. ports. The U.S. program has been instrumental in raising sanitation standards aboard **cruise ships,** notably in food handling, food preparation, and water quality in pools and spas. CDC has also issued advisory guidelines for sanitation-related design elements for new **cruise ships** as well as operational guidelines for pools and spas.

Centrum
The term used for atrium by Royal Caribbean International aboard ship. Coined by Rod McLeod for use aboard *Sovereign of the Seas*, the first **megaship**, it was inspired by the Norwegian practice of referring to the downtown area as the centrum.

Certificate of Class for Machinery and Equipment
See **Class**.

Certificate of Compliance with ILO Crew Accommodation Regulation

Issued by the ship's country of **administration** or **classification society**, this certificate affirms that the standard for crew accommodation is in compliance with **International Labor Organization** minimum standards.

Certificate of Nationality

See **Class.**

Certificate of Registry

A document issued by flag **administration** confirming the name of the ship, date of construction, **gross** and **net tonnage, length overall, registry, call sign, master**, owner(s) and other relevant information. The certificate is reissued whenever a ship changes hands. It must be presented on entering a **port**.

Certificate of Survey

A certificate that is issued by a **classification society** through **surveyors** whom the society has appointed to inspect a vessel. If a ship has been damaged, a port authority may request a survey. Certificates of survey are also issued periodically Examples: when a vessel is **drydocked** for overhaul; when a major refit or renovation has taken place; and when annual surveys, or other types of survey, are conducted for any reason.

Chart

For the sea what a map is for the land, except that charts need to be more precise than most maps. They show ocean depth, the contour of the ocean floor, and the height of adjacent land masses. There is also a variety of relevant information about the sea: locations of buoys, information about port approaches and channels, rivers, positions of lighthouses, wreck locations, and other vital information. Charts are issued by the hydrographic departments of various nations and are regularly updated.

Charter

Also referred to as a full-ship charter, the term is used when a vessel is chartered to an organization for one or more complete sailings. These sailings are then not for sale to the public at large. This becomes an attractive option for organizing sales incentive groups; for special-interest sailings; or for those catering to one group of passengers. Special entertainment features can be organized without offense to non-group passengers. There is much more flexibility for on board activities than is the case with even a large group aboard a normal sailing. Food and other amenities can be negotiated for upgrade. Frequently, charters are undertaken on the vessel's normal route. However, departures from the usual itinerary are usually possible with or without additional cost.

There are various other types of charter. A **time charter** involves hire of a vessel for a specific period of time; a **voyage charter** for one cruise, on or off a vessel's regular run; a **bareboat charter**, generally for a longer period, means that the charterer takes the ship and supplies everything needed for a vessel's operation; a **partial charter** or **part-ship charter** is used to describe hiring part of a ship's capacity for selected voyages, a season, a year, or longer; a **charter purchase** is a lease-purchase arrangement; a **charter back** deal occurs when a cruise line sells a ship, then charters it back – perhaps to raise money or to meet previous commitments.

Charter Back

Where the owner of a vessel sells a ship and the vessel is already committed for a period of time, the seller will often charter back the vessel from the new owner until the agreed upon delivery date of the ship. The reason for such a future delivery is to allow both the seller and the buyer to lock in a price but defer the actual exchange of property. A charter back may also be arranged when a company wishes to restructure its debt. In this instance, the cruise line sells the vessel to a financial institution or another company and then charters it back. Such a transaction may also be prompted by tax or other regulatory requirements. See also **Charter**.

Charter Party

Contract, or deed, for a **charter**.

Dictionary of the Cruise Industry

Charter Purchase

A lease-purchase agreement applied to a ship. Part of the charter fees are applied to the purchase price of the vessel. The price of the ship is agreed to in advance, and there is a predetermined date when the transfer of ownership occurs. At times, a general charter agreement may be converted into a charter purchase.

Checker

Longshoreman that checks deliveries to the ship.

Chief Engineer

Officer with ultimate responsibility for propulsion and other machinery aboard ship.

Chief Officer

See **Staff Captain.**

Chief Purser

Over most of the history of ocean travel, the Chief Purser has been the senior official on board concerned with financial administration and through this, in the early days of ocean travel, hotel operations – the need to buy food, pay staff, and handle the money of passengers. In many lines, this title has been replaced by Hotel Manager. In others, the position has been retained to deal with financial matters such as payroll, purchases that passengers make through concessionaires, currency exchange services, etc. Aboard some **cruise ships,** the Chief Purser still is the senior individual on board dealing with hotel operations. In other ships, purser responsibilities are divided with individuals responsible for dealing with the public, with crew, etc. There is no firm rule on purser responsibilities, just a general connection with money and hotel operation.

Chief Steward

A traditional shipboard position, this job title is used variously by different companies. Originally, the Chief Steward was the person in charge of all the food and beverage services. As one current example, aboard Carnival Cruise Lines the Chief Steward is the equivalent of housekeeping manager and is in charge of the cleanliness of the ship. On Greek vessels, the Chief Steward is in charge of food service and housekeeping. In both cases, the Chief Steward is not a senior officer as in the old days but one of several staff coordinating a segment of hotel operations.

Christening or Naming Ceremony

Traditionally, the naming ceremony of a vessel took place in the shipyard at time of launching and was, for most companies, a high ceremonial occasion. This was in the days when ships were launched from inclined building ways, itself a fairly dramatic process. Now, a vessel is usually built in a drydock and merely floated out in surroundings that resemble a factory yard. A ceremonial scoop is taken of the first water to touch the hull. While Christening or naming ceremonies (which term is used seems to depend on whether the management is Christian or of another religion) sometimes take place at shipyards, most often they are organized to coincide with the vessel's first visit to the initial home port from which the ship will operate – and close to major media markets. The ceremony may include a blessing of the vessel by a priest, but invariably the owners and local dignitaries are featured and the press is invited. As in the days when ships were named at time of launching, a bottle of champagne is broken over the **bow** of the ship. The person who was formerly called the vessel's **sponsor** (the individual naming the ship) is now frequently called the **Godmother**. By tradition, it is almost always a woman and, in current practice, a celebrity. Sometimes, there is a simultaneous unveiling of the vessel's name. Like the traditional sponsor, the Godmother may well feel an affiliation with the ship that lasts through the lifetime of both.

Civil Aviation Authority

The UK body governing the sale of airline tickets, including those sold as part of fly/cruise packages.

Class

(1) A group of vessels built to the same, or virtually

the same, design. Two well-known examples are the *Fantasy* Class, one of the largest classes of ships ever built in the history of commercial passenger shipping; and the *Statendam* Class, after the first of four nearly identical ships built for Holland America. (2) A vessel is referred to as being **in class** when the ship complies with all the international safety requirements issued by the **IMO** for the type of ship e.g. **cruise ship,** tanker, ferry. A certificate of being in class is issued by the **classification society** with jurisdiction over the ship (**Lloyd's Register**, etc.). Vessel's sale transaction almost always makes reference to a vessel being in class upon delivery. (3) When passenger ships were used primarily for point-to-point transportation, they usually had more than one class of accommodation. Each class was virtually a ship within a ship, with its own dining room, lounges, and deck areas. There was generally rigid separation of the classes. The class structure of vessels on a given run tended to reflect the social structure of those travelling, with as many as four classes but more often, two or three. When these same ships were used in one-class cruising, the amount of redundant space and the number of unsuitable (e.g. third class) **cabins** made cruising most often a loss-reducing rather than a profitable enterprise in the early days. *QE2* was a transitional ship in the history of class structure: originally conceived as a three class ship (first, cabin, and tourist), by the time it entered service there were just two classes but with all passengers enjoying run-of-ship privileges. However, the dining room to which passengers were assigned, even on cruises, varied with the fare paid. More elaborate a-la-carte dining was available in dining rooms for passengers paying higher fares.

Classic Cruise Ship

Refers to passenger ships designed primarily for point-to-point transportation, with few exceptions in the 1960's or earlier. These are characterized by the curvaceous lines used in the days before extensive prefabrication in shipbuilding, by deep **keels** resulting in deeper **draft**, by **portholes** in the hull rather than windows, and prior to the 1960's, by rivetted **hull** construction. These usually had multiple cabin types due to the complex shape of the vessel. Many of these ships had a sleekness necessary not for aesthetic reasons but in order for the ship to maintain a regular schedule in conditions of rough weather and high wind. This required a sleek hull shape. Most were strongly built with rigid hull construction and thick metal plates, something that has contributed to their longevity. Often, engines and other equipment have been replaced to make these efficient and profitable cruise ships. As part of **conversion** to cruise status, new **cabins** are often built into public rooms originally intended for second or third class. Cabins intended for lower classes are sometimes ripped out in favor of modern, standard cruise ship accommodation. This can be a challenge as when the former Grace liner *Santa Rosa* was converted into the cruise ship *Regent Rainbow*. The new owners fitted standard cabins, manufactured in a factory separate from the ship, into the vessel's curved hull. Other classic **cruise ships** that have undergone some degree of conversion: Premier Cruise Line's *IslandBreeze* (ex-*Festivale*, ex-*Transvaal Castle*), Premier's *Seawind Crown* (ex-*Vasco da Gama*) and *OceanBreeze* (originally *Southern Cross*), NCL's *Norway* (ex-*France*), and others.

Classification Society

A private agency recognized by the **IMO** as well as by a variety of insurance companies, underwriters and other national and international organizations as qualified and able to certify elements of vessel construction relating to **seaworthiness** and general safety. For a vessel to take cargo or passengers or to enter or leave a **port**, valid insurance as well as a **certificate of compliance** with specific international **conventions** is required. A vessel cannot obtain insurance without having the vessel's construction, subsequent **conversions,** current condition and procedures regarding safety certified by the classification society. Among several large classification societies: **Lloyd's Register of Shipping** of Great Britain; **Det Norske Veritas (DNV)** of Norway; **Germanischer Lloyd** of

Germany; and others. The Classification Society follows design and construction throughout both processes, and the ship's subsequent history through conversions, if any, until the ship is sold for **scrap**. The **Classification Society** also certifies the **class** of the vessel which will depend on the type of operation envisioned for it and design attributes provided. A ship intended for operation in the Caribbean will be built to a different class than one that will offer cruises deep into the Arctic and Antarctic.

Clear the Vessel

Before passengers and **crew** can **disembark** on arrival from or in a foreign **port**, local authorities need to clear the vessel. Depending on local regulations and circumstances surrounding the arrival of the ship, the procedure can include participation by immigration, customs, **port authority, coast guard, Center for Disease Control (CDC)**, and other authorities.

CLIA

See **Cruise Lines International Association**.

Co-op Advertising

When a cruise line shares the cost of advertising including TV spots, special brochures, or other publicity, with a travel agency.

Coastwise Shipping Laws

See **Cabotage**.

COGES (Combined Gas Turbine and Steam Turbine Integrated Electric Drive Propulsion System)

See **Gas Turbine**.

Coin Under the Mast

An old Finnish tradition also common in other Scandinavian countries and in Europe, it involves putting a coin under the mast of a vessel during construction. This, according to legend, will ensure that the ship will sail safely in calm seas. This practice has existed for about 2,000 years. Although modern vessels do not have a mast in the traditional sense, the ceremony is nevertheless performed when vessels are constructed in Scandinavian yards. The owners are invited and a coin is placed under a welded steel plate on the

Collateral Material

One term for publicity material including brochures, pamphlets, post cards, videos, posters, etc. that a cruise line produces to promote itself.

Combined Gas Turbine and Steam Turbine Integrated Electric Drive Propulsion System

See **Gas Turbine.**

Combivessel

Often referred to as a passenger-cargo ship, this is a vessel that carries more than twelve passengers in addition to cargo. These are rare because of conflicting requirements of passengers (for a strict schedule) and cargo (where schedule flexibility is important due to varying amounts of cargo to be loaded/unloaded and delays in arrival of goods being shipped). In practice, the demands of cargo often take precedence over passenger considerations in such matters as port time. When vessels were mainly point-to-point transportation, almost all passenger ships, even the largest, carried limited or moderate amounts of cargo. This was practical because stays in terminal ports of two or more days were common and personnel costs were much lower than they are now. The best-known combivessel now operating is Ivaran Line's *Americana*, a container vessel with high-grade accommodation for eighty-eight passengers. One of the largest passenger ships with major cargo capacity was Shaw Savill's 1939 *Dominion Monarch*, 27,155 tons with first class accommodation for 517 passengers. Northbound passengers on the Australia/New Zealand run shared the vessel with thousands of tons of chilled meat carcasses. It is significant that the next major passenger ship built for the line, the 20,204-ton *Southern Cross* of 1955, was the first ocean **liner** to carry no cargo. At the time, the line cited the above conflicting requirements. Other lines that used to combine huge cargo capacity with accommodation for hundreds of passengers: Royal Mail Line (Britain-East Coast of South America), Union Castle Line (Britain-South and East Africa), British India (Britain, East Africa, and the Orient), and Messagerie Maritimes (worldwide, the French equivalent of P & O). Several former combivessels still operate as **cruise ships.** Among them: the former *Transvaal Castle*, later *Festivale* and now *IslandBreeze*; Mediterranean Shipping's *Monterey*, formerly sailing for Matson Lines under the same name with just 365 passengers and a great deal of cargo; and *Princesa Victoria*, originally Union Castle's *Dunnottar Castle*. The United States constructed major fleets of combivessels before and just after World War II. The combivessels of lines such as American President, Delta, Farrel, and Grace were well-known, and sailings were frequently marketed as cruises. American combivessels usually carried about a hundred passengers or less.

Comment Cards

Comment cards reflect passengers' satisfaction, or dissatisfaction, with a cruise. The cards are studied closely by shore-side management and in some cruise lines, aboard ship, as a significant instrument for quality control. They are used for a variety of purposes. They can request information to construct a passenger profile – age, repeat passenger status, and other individual information, and may also be tied to a bonus system for waiters or cabin stewards to reward those who do a fine job of pleasing passengers. In comparison with hotels, top management is more removed from the customer aboard a ship at sea, especially when the ship is based some distance from the home office. It is therefore important that a major percentage of passengers complete the cards. To secure a high return, passengers who submit comment cards have the chance to win prizes. Final drawing takes place minutes before disembarkation.

Commission Cap

Maximum commission paid to an individual agent by policy, expressed in a dollar amount, regardless of established percentage of commission. This practice was initiated by many airlines in early 1995, and later, by Renaissance Cruises.

Commission Policy

Relates to commissions paid to travel agents for

booking clients on a cruise. and the schedule for such payment. Each line has its own policy on commission level. These vary, but commonly begin at 10%. However, **overrides** within a tiered commission structure are almost always available for a company's high-volume producers among the agent community or by special agreement. There is also a commission policy relating to when commissions are paid. If the deposit or fare is paid in cash, the travel agent usually retains the commission portion. However, when a travel agent pays for the cruise with a customer's credit card (as in most cases for bookings made in North America), the commission to the travel agent is paid by the cruise line. Some 1997 policies for when commission is paid: Carnival, RCCL, and Princess pay when the customer makes full payment for the cruise. Royal Olympic Cruises pays four weeks after the client returns from the cruise. Orient, Renaissance, and Radisson also pay after the cruise is over.

Commission Rate on Bookings
See **Commission Policy.**

Comp
Complimentary, referring to cruise passage or cruise amenities provided *gratis* to writers or tour leaders. "Comp" passage for the latter are provided for in a line's group policy and negotiated as part of group agreements. Also used commonly as a verb, e.g. "comp" or "comped." Cruises, and frequently shore excursions, are often provided on a complimentary basis to writers. Less frequently, other amenities may be "comped" for writers, tour organizers, and VIP's on board.

Compartment
(1) Watertight subdivision within a ship designed to keep the ship afloat even though other compartments are damaged; (2) any compartment within a ship. Generally, compartments within a merchant ship represent the distance between transverse watertight bulkheads, or walls. Further subdivision of a **cruise ship**, aside from ballast and fuel tanks, is not considered advisable because flooding on one side of the vessel may cause the ship to lose stability and cause it to capsize.

Dictionary of the Cruise Industry

Compartments, Maximum Permissible Length
As used in **SOLAS**, the maximum permissible length of any compartment is the **floodable length** multiplied by the **factor of subdivision**, the latter depending on the length of the ship and the nature of service for which it is intended.

Concessionaire
The operator of a service on board a ship by a firm not owned or operated by a cruise line. This is most commonly applied to firms offering services to passengers such as food and bar service, photography, shops, etc., though occasionally both officers and crew can be on a concessionaire basis.

Condition of Class
Usually, a known defect that is not considered serious enough to prevent a ship from sailing. A condition of class states the date by which repairs must be made.

Consolidation
An industry trend that originated in the 1980's and accelerated in the 1990's, consolidation is the tendency of small cruise lines to be purchased by larger companies. The trend gained momentum with the realization that the future of the industry belongs to those with capital to build new ships, especially **megaships**. The strong, consolidated company, aided by public stock offerings, is able to order these vessels in quantity, marshall strong and effective multimedia advertising, maintain large sales forces in the field, and achieve the major profits that are available in today's marketplace. Early, fairly unsuccessful efforts at consolidation included the acquisition of Royal Viking Line and Royal Cruise Line by NCL. Later, acquisition of Sitmar by Princess helped the latter to grow more quickly and become one of the three major cruise lines dominating the industry. Another early and extremely successful consolidation was Carnival's acquisition of Holland America Cruises followed by the purchase of controlling interest in Seabourn, Airtours, Costa, and Cunard. Royal Caribbean ensured its continuance as one of the "big three" by acquiring Admiral Cruises and, more recently, Celebrity. Aside from Princess's acquisition of

Sitmar, the most successful consolidations have involved maintaining and improving the distinct separate branding of lines acquired while providing capital for their expansion.

Construction Date

The actual date that the first sections of metal are put in place in the drydock where a ship is being constructed, beginning the fabrication of a vessel. In the days of ocean **liners**, this was referred to as the laying of the **keel** and meant putting in place on the **ways** the first section of the backbone of the ship.

Constructive Total Loss.

A damaged ship's status where the cost of repair is greater than the value of the vessel.

Consumables

Commodities throughout the ship consumed in the operation of the vessel, excluding food and beverage items. Consumables must be counted and paid for at cost when a vessel is chartered or sold. Where items are purchased in containers, these must be unopened.

Contemporary Cruise Market Segment

See **Mass Market.**

Contiguous Zone

Sometimes known as the **adjacent zone,** this is the area immediately beyond territorial waters. According to the Law of the Sea Convention, Article 33(2), the Contiguous Zone may not extend beyond twenty-four miles from the baseline (a line determined by measuring the low water line).

Contraband

Prohibited cargo – such as goods being smuggled, or illegal commodities transported aboard a passenger ship.

Contract

See **Seafarer's Agreement.**

Control Stations

As used in **SOLAS,** the spaces housing the vessel's radio, main navigating equipment, emergency power source, or centralized fire recording or fire control equipment.

Controllable Pitch Propellers

Propellers where the angle of blades can be adjusted to change the speed or direction of a vessel without changing engine, or propeller shaft speed. These eliminate the need for gearing otherwise required to handle the difference in engine RPM's and those of the propeller. They also allow high-skew blades to be employed which, if correctly designed, can minimize vibration and pressure pulses.

Conversion

Renovation of a ship that is intended to make it suitable for another type of operation. Most common in the cruise industry is conversion of a cargo or combination cargo/passenger vessel to all-passenger status. Good examples of combination ship conversions are the rebuilding of the Union Castle Line passenger/cargo ship *Transvaal Castle* into the Carnival **Cruise ship** *Festivale*; and several cargo ship conversions, including the creation of the Costa **Cruise ships** *CostaMarina* and *CostaAllegra* into highly successful modern **cruise ships** from the containerships *Axel Johnson* and *Annie Johnson* respectively. What emerged from the Carnival conversion was the ship that was responsible for the line's initial runaway success; and in the Costa ships, attractive, modern, and versatile **cruise ships** with high-quality accommodation. Conversion can be an attractive option for producing a new **cruise ship** provided financing opportunities and the availability of a suitable ship to convert do not undermine the cost advantages.

Convertible Lower Beds

(1) Two lower single beds convertible to a double, usually of king size; (2) lower bed(s) convertible to settee(s). In some cases, the beds may be convertible into both. However, if luggage is stored underneath, it becomes awkward to move these beds once the initial arrangement has been made. In the immediate post-war era, the phrase "living room by day, bedroom by night" was a catch-phrase widely used to advertise convertible capability aboard American ships. At the time, the ability to convert to double - or queen-bed status was rare since

berths were usually fixed to the structure of the ship and could not be moved.

Corrosion-Resistant
A painted or other surface that remains intact in spite of prolonged exposure to operating or other environmental conditions.

Country of Registry
See **Administration**.

Crash Stop
Sudden reversal of engines or propeller pitch as applicable to produce full power astern and bring the vessel to a stop, generally in an emergency situation.

Credit Watch
When a credit rating agency places an alert on a cruise line for the benefit of those proposing to purchase bonds of the company. Such factors as major operating losses or operational problems could trigger such a watch.

Crew
Expression used loosely to describe the total number of people working on a vessel. The term actually embraces a variety of categories such as officers, deck and engine personnel, cabin stewards and catering staff, concessionaires and others depending on the line.

Crew Administration
A shore side department that is responsible for matters relating to the hiring, work, and termination of crew. The department's responsibilities include recruiting, administering medical testing prior to boarding, arranging for crew travel to and from the vessel, and other matters. In some companies this department is also involved in crew payroll administration; in others there is a separation and payroll is part of accounting. This is a complex area that merits a separate department.

Crew Bar
A bar aboard the vessel for the exclusive use of crew members. The crew bar sells alcoholic beverages at a discount to crew and is an important recreation area for ship's staff. Depending on the ship and company, the crew bar includes such

entertainment elements as television, VCR, pinball machines, etc.

Crew Mess
The crew's dining room on board a vessel. In modern **cruise ships,** there are a number of crew messes. While there is always a separate dining room for the captain and officers, the degree of dining room separation among other ranks varies a great deal. On large ships, it is not uncommon to have six dining rooms for ship's crew.

Crew Purser
A purser on board the vessel in charge of financial relations with the **crew** including payroll, loans, and on board charges. The Crew Purser may also be responsible for maintaining the personnel files of crew members, including passport and immigration papers.

Crewing Agency
A private company that specializes in providing crews for ships. Some specialize in the **deck and engine** areas, others in the hotel side of **cruise ship** operation. Certain agencies just recruit, others provide training as well.

Critical Sailing Index (CSI)
A cruise line's sailing list annotated with yield management information, dividing the list according to demand. The CSI indicates to management which sailings require no further incentives (i.e. deeper discounts) and which are likely to fill at current and anticipated booking rates.

Croisimer
The French equivalent of **Cruise Lines International Association (CLIA)** in the United States and the **Passenger Shipping Association (PSA)** in the U.K., i.e. a trade association founded in 1970 to re-energize the French cruise market. The organization is involved in cruise promotion and agent training in France.

Crossing the Line
The occasion for a ceremony in which passengers and crew crossing the Equator for the first time are initiated in a ceremony presided over by the mythical King Neptune. Aboard **cruise ships,** this is the

occasion for initiates to be tossed in the ship's swimming pool, covered with soap or lather, and/or to suffer other indignities. As one might expect in this suit-minded age, participation is voluntary.

Crow's Nest

In the days of the great liners, this was a lookout post high in the foremast intended to supplement the lookout on the bridge. The name has been applied, almost generically, to observation lounge/bars located high up and forward above the bridge. Such venues offer scenic views but often are underutilized since they tend to be away from normal passenger circulation patterns aboard ship. They are, of course, well-populated on entering and leaving port. Some cruise lines have compensated for this tendency toward underutilization by giving to these rooms additional functions – lecture, disco, or private entertaining areas (as on Holland America's *Statendam* Class), or casino (*Crown* and *Regal Princess*).

Cruise and Stay Vacation

A vacation where a cruise is packaged and sold along with extensive land and sometimes, air arrangements. The difference between these trips and the typical pre- and post-cruise packages is that the cruise is equally or less important than land arrangements. Cruise and stay vacations are often sold in destination-rich areas such as the Mediterranean where a week in a hotel is often packaged as part of a one-week cruise in the low-cost segment of the Mediterranean-based cruise industry. Other examples include stays at Disney World combined with cruises from Port Canaveral and South Florida, and the practice by South Florida daycruise operators of packaging hotel stays in Freeport with Miami/Fort Lauderdale - Freeport daycruise offerings. In European waters, such packaging is frequently undertaken by passenger ferry operators. See also **Pre- and Post-**

Cruise Packages. This practice is not common in the Caribbean where the current market supports sell-outs for the entire cruise and where, unlike in the Mediterranean, quality economy hotel accommodation ashore is more difficult to find with the volume necessary to support a cruise and stay operation.

Cruise Areas

Locale that constitutes a distinct cruise market, e.g. the Caribbean, Mediterranean, Baltic, and Far East. In Europe, the term "cruising grounds" is sometimes used. The busiest include the Caribbean, the Mediterranean, Alaska, Mexican Riviera, **Transcanal**, the Baltic, Norwegian fjords (the latter two frequently combined as "Northern European"), South Africa/Indian Ocean, South Asia, North Asia, South American (not always divided by area around that continent), and others.

Cruise Attributes

This term is used in the process of breaking down the components of the generic cruise experience in order to analyze the relationship of the over-all experience to passenger expectations. Attributes include value, all-inclusiveness, the romance factor, not having to pack and unpack at each destination, price predictability, etc.

Cruise Brand

A cruise line with a separate name, though not necessarily separate ownership from other companies or entities. A cruise brand usually represents ships with a single standard of accommodation and most often, cruising style. An example of a stand-alone cruise brand is Commodore Cruise Lines. Examples of cruise brands owned by parent cruise corporations with more than one cruise brand are Holland America, Costa Cruises, Celebrity, and Orient. To achieve proper identity in the market place, the cruise experience ought to be predictable and of a comprehensible, uniform standard, as implied in the concept "cruise brand." When this is not the case, there is trouble.

Cruise Counselor

A travel agent who specializes in selling cruise vacations. **CLIA** has introduced cruise counselor certification programs training travel agents in the selling of cruise vacations.

Cruise Director

The person in charge of entertainment and organized passenger activities on board a **cruise ship.** The Cruise Director plans and issues the daily activity program, coordinates all entertainment, and serves as the passengers' liaison with the captain and management of the vessel, and often supervises the sale of shore excursions and serves as the ship-board interface with excursion operators. In the modern cruise industry, this is one of the most powerful and best-paying positions aboard ship. Cruise directors can make or break the on board ambiance. The practice of having a cruise director, especially one with far-reaching authority and responsibility, developed gradually with the industry itself. In the 1930's, it was common to have a host or hostess. As full-time cruise employment for ships became common, the practice became more universal. Many cruise directors got their start in show business and become part of a ship's entertainment program. Many others, some with show business backgrounds, first worked aboard ship in the Sixties and Seventies when Great Britain possessed a major fleet of **cruise ships,** most of them former liners. Thus, for years **cruise ships** based in the United States fielded cruise directors with British accents. Whatever the accent, the cruise director does much to set the tone of a cruise experience. Cruise Director is also the name of American Airlines' computerized cruise reservation system, a part of SABRE.

Cruise Documents

Set of documents received by a passenger prior to sailing. This typically includes the cruise and air line tickets, a pre-cruise information booklet ("What to know before you go" or similar), luggage tags, information on shore excursions, and at times other items.

Cruise Europe

A major association of European ports of call with sixty-six members at time of writing. Major coverage is Europe outside the Mediterranean. The

Dictionary of the Cruise Industry

Cruise Line Impact Study

purpose of this regional cruise association is to promote members as ports of call.

Cruise Line Impact Study

Commissioned by the **Florida Caribbean Cruise Association (FCCA)** in 1992 and annually since then to assess the economic impact of the cruise industry on Caribbean countries. It arose from the claim by some islands and the Caribbean hotel industry in general that **cruise ships** were not contributing to the economy and that port taxes/fees should be increased. The Study has provided important information on the industry's impact on the Caribbean and is utilized by investors assessing cruise-related projects in the area.

Cruise Lines International Association (CLIA)

An international trade association of cruise lines active in the North American market. Its activities include promoting the cruise industry as well as training and certifying travel agency personnel. Travel agencies that are CLIA-affiliated employ Accredited Cruise Counsellors (ACC's) and Master Cruise Counsellors (MCC's) who are highly trained by CLIA in their understanding as to what each cruise line has to offer. This training of travel agents is done through first-hand experience (ship inspections and actual cruises) and specifically targeted training programs (such as Principles of Professional Selling and Effective Presentation Skills). A major barrier to the growth of the industry has been lack of knowledge of cruise products by travel agent personnel. There is often a high turnover rate in the latter, which multiplies the difficulty. Thus, CLIA performs an important service for cruise lines active in the North American market. CLIA also promotes generic cruise advertising underwritten by the membership. This is aimed at increasing the number of people who take cruises in North America.

Cruise Night

Sales event, sponsored jointly by a cruise line district sales manager and travel agent, inviting prospective cruise clients to a hotel or home to discuss cruises. Refreshments are served, there are questions and answers, and the result is an effective sales technique.

Cruise Only
A cruise sold exclusive of airfare or pre- and post-cruise vacation packages. If the price of a cruise includes airfare, a credit is frequently available to cruise-only passengers.

Cruise Region
See **Cruise Area**.

Cruise Revenue
The revenues attributed to the cruise exclusive of any **add ons** such as air revenue, insurance, or other elements. Most large cruise lines, in their financial reports, include all revenues attributed to the vessel operation as cruise revenue. i.e., port charges and on board revenue. There is little standardization in the industry on how this is handled.

Cruise Segments
A product of air/sea packaging, cruise lines tend to sell parts of a longer cruise inclusive of air transportation and, sometimes, of hotel and other land arrangements. This is most frequently done in the case of world or extended cruises where it is unlikely that the voyage will be completely sold to passengers taking the entire cruise. Often segmented are cruises around South America, which take in excess of fifty days and lend themselves to such segmentation. Typical segments: U.S. to Rio de Janeiro; Rio to Buenos Aires; BA to Valparaiso, Chile; and Valparaiso to U.S., this last a long segment sometimes subdivided further. World Cruises are often segmented, though these voyages tend to be social and segmentees can find themselves outside the "in" group in the social pecking order. Another example of segmentation is the Mediterranean **cruise and stay** packages sold in the European market.

Cruise Ship
(1) A ship used for cruises; (2) a ship built primarily or exclusively for cruising. The following are characteristics of most recent ships built expressly for cruising: uniform standards of accommodation throughout, except for some deluxe accommodation; shallow **draft**, usually twenty-six feet or less; built with warm-water cruising in mind, though frequently found in northern waters in the

Cruise Ship

warm-weather season; extensive areas for sunning; broad, as opposed to fine, **hull** lines; usually, with speeds of twenty-two knots or less. Cruise ships have hull plating (see **scantlings**) and hull lines that reflect their good-weather deployment for most of the year. The general design of the modern cruise ship has evolved from both ocean **liners** and the modern **carferry**. The first generation of new, diesel-driven cruise ships owed more to the **carferry** side of the design heritage. The *Starward* demonstrated that it was possible to build a profitable new ship with a high average standard of accommodation and make a great deal of money in cruise service. *Starward*, one of the first modern cruise ships built for the trade from South Florida, actually had a garage and carried trucks to and from Jamaica in her early years. Cabins reflected the carferry heritage and were small – little more than 120 square feet per passenger. Gradually, cruise ships began to incorporate more of the traditional comforts of ocean travel in their design. They became more spacious, offered more varied public areas, and evolved into the **megaship** of today. The tradition and nostalgia of ocean **liners** have contributed much to the modern concept of the cruise ship at its best. During the Twentieth Century, and especially after World War I, ocean **liners** were increasingly used in cruise service and gradually incorporated cruise features in their design. The first major dual-purpose liner, designed to cruise in winter and sail the North Atlantic in summer, was Canadian Pacific's 1931 *Empress of Britain*. Her **world cruises** contributed much to the legend and lore of cruising. Cunard's *Caronia* of 1948, designed as a dual-purpose ship, spent almost all her time on cruises and is said to have offered the best food and service ever provided by the line. Most of the postwar ships of Norwegian America Line and Swedish America Line, with mostly large outside cabins and low passenger capacities for their size, were designed perhaps more for cruises than for Atlantic Service. With the notable exception of the major Atlantic liners of the Italian and French Line, all new passenger ships of the late 1950's and 1960's were designed with cruising in mind. Even those not so conceived – *France*, *Leonardo da Vinci*, *Michelangelo*, and *Raffaello*, cruised in their later years, sometimes on a full-time basis. Drawbacks for Atlantic liners used as cruise ships: multi-class systems leading to dramatically contrasting standards of accommodation throughout the ship; excessively deep draft; closed-in design with decks that were not always hospitable in warm weather; inability to cruise efficiency at reduced speed. Strong point: the legend and romance of ocean travel that they brought to cruising, earned on the basis of their best accommodation. While the modern cruise ship has its ancestry in the Baltic ferry, the first ship built exclusively for cruising was the *Prinzessin Victoria Luise*, 4429 gross tons, built for the Hamburg America Line (Hapag) in 1900.

Cruise Specialist
See **Cruise Counselor**.

Cruise Staff
Crew members on board ship that assist the **cruise director** with on board activities and entertainment. Common positions include hostess, shore excursion manager, assistant cruise director, and other designations. Frequently, members of the cruise staff double as entertainers, especially dancers.

Cruise Terminal
Building where passengers embark, disembark, or go ashore if the terminal is located in a cruise port of call. Many terminals must be designed with the needs of both originating and transit passengers in mind. Among those that handle large numbers of both originating and transit passengers are facilities San Juan, Barbados, and Piraeus, port for Athens, Greece. Embarking and disembarking passenger baggage in a setting protected from the elements has an impact on cruise terminal design that is additional to that required for transit passengers.

Cruise to Nowhere
A cruise without a port of call that returns to the port of departure. In the United States, the typical cruise to nowhere goes outside U.S. territorial waters and returns to the port of embarkation. Foreign-flag vessels not stopping at a foreign port

must leave territorial waters to have gaming on board. There are three types of cruises to nowhere in existence today: (1) one or two-night cruises using traditional vessels where the appeal is a brief offshore escape and, to a lesser extent, gaming; (2) pre-inaugural trips by new, newly purchased, or newly refitted ships with non-revenue passengers, usually travel agents, travel press, and other guests of the line; and (3) day cruises, most of them in North American waters, the mainstay of which is gambling but which also feature the traditional shipboard attractions of food and entertainment. Cruises in the first category are often scheduled along with four- and five-night sailings to create a weekly cruise cycle. They attract such traditional vessels as Regal Cruises' *Regal Empress* and Carnival Cruises' new giantess, *Carnival Triumph*. Major vessels often carry tens of thousands of pre-inaugural passengers when they are introduced into service. The third category attracts ships of many sizes usually ranging from vessels the size of large excursion boats to those resembling European ferries which, in some cases, was their former operating status.

Cruise Tour

A package that combines a tour and a cruise. This term is usually used when there is a substantial shore portion – more than two days. If a **pre-** or **post-cruise** hotel stay of one to three nights is purchased through the cruise line, this normally does not justify use of this term unless the hotel stays are an integral part of the cruise package, not an extra-cost option. Among the well-known cruise tours are those operated in Alaska by Princess, Holland America, and other companies.

Cruise-Oriented Agency

A travel agency specializing in selling cruise vacations and packages inclusive of cruisers. A trade association of such agencies, the National Association of Cruise-Oriented Agencies (NCOA), has been established to represent the interest of its members vis-a-vis the cruise industry and government.

Cruisevoy

Standard **charter party** form developed by the Copenhagen-based international shipping association BIMCO. First published in April, 1998, this voyage or "trip" charter party is intended to cover the relationship between the owner of a **cruise ship** and a tour operator, travel bureau, or large corporation planning an incentive cruise for its staff. BIMCO's documentary committee is considering future development of a long-time charter party for **cruise ships**.

Cruising Grounds

See **Cruise Areas**.

Cruising Speed

(1) The speed at which a vessel normally operates; or (2) the maximum sustained sea speed of which a ship is capable for an indefinite period. The speed indicated by (2) normally applies to the speed a ship can maintain with one engine (motorships) or one boiler (steamships) not in use that is available for routine maintenance. Almost all ships can maintain higher speeds for short periods with all engines or boilers online. However, in the modern cruise industry where ships are normally in operation seven nights each week, with even overnight stays unusual, this is not the realistic sustained maximum. Interport speeds of passenger ships have always varied greatly and are calculated to allow for morning arrivals and evening departures. If a ship is sailing from Miami to Nassau, thirteen knots is generally sufficient. On the other hand, the direct Miami-San Juan leg is usually made at maximum sustained sea speed to allow for arrival as early on the third day as possible. Here, the higher speeds built into some modern **cruise ships** would convert this traditional night life stop into one with both day and evening attractions. Pacific and some Mediterranean itineraries can also be more varied if the ship has a maximum sustained sea speed of 24 or 25 knots rather than the typical 19 - 21. The cruising speed is the one normally advertised by the cruise line and featured in cruise publications, generally the maximum sustainable for a long period.

CSI
See **Critical Sailing Index**.

D

Damage Control Plan
According to **SOLAS**, plans must show the various decks, watertight compartments, all openings in them and the position of closure controls, and arrangements for eliminating lists due to flooding. Booklets containing this same information should be made available to officers, and the plan should be posted in a conspicuous place e.g. on the bridge.

Davit
The steel arms that secure in place a lifeboat when stored aboard ship, and lowers it when this is required. Prior to the age of **megaships**, davits containing lifeboats were usually mounted high in the **superstructure**. Now, with encouragement by **SOLAS**, lifeboats are most often stored in recesses lower in the ship but above the **hull** in what is a midpoint in the passenger accommodation. The first ships to employ this configuration were Hamburg America's *Imperator* class transatlantic superliners that entered service starting in 1913. The arrangement was also used in the Dutch *Oranje* and *Willem Ruys*, both designed just prior to World War II. The practice was revived in two large, fast British ships that entered service in 1960 and 1961, P & O's *Oriana* and *Canberra*. Recesses provide a much more protected location from which to launch boats in the event of an emergency, and provide for less lowering distance between the point where passengers and crew embark and the water. At the same time, the weight that these represent is lower in the ship, something that contributes to better stability. The latest amendments to SOLAS specify in meters the height at which lifeboats may be mounted.

Day Cruises
Cruises lasting a day or less which may or may not have a port of call. These are popular in many areas of the world. The number of day cruises has expanded dramatically in the United States due to

changes in gaming laws which allow gambling on U.S.-flag vessels inside territorial waters unless otherwise prohibited by state law (non-U.S. ships offer gambling on day cruises but must leave territorial waters). The cruises also provide a brief offshore escape at low cost. Day cruises in European waters have been popular for many years. A good example are those from Athens to the Saronic Gulf which offer interesting ports of call and return within twelve hours. European day cruises often employ ships comparable in size to those used for gambling and entertainment cruises from U.S. ports.

Days in the Market

This measure is commonly used to profile the operations of a cruise line within a given region. The term also applies if operating limitations are attached in the course of a ship sale (see also **Trading Limitations**). If a ship is sold with operating conditions and limitations attached (e.g. no more than 100 days each year in the Caribbean market), "days in the market" is a useful measure. More frequently, it is used to describe the operating focus of an entire fleet.

Dead Ship

Main propulsion plant, boilers (if any), and auxiliaries are not in operation. When a ship loses power, the vessel is commonly referred to as a "dead" ship.

Dead Ship Condition

SOLAS term for the condition where, due to the absence of power, the main propulsion plant, boilers and auxiliaries are not functioning.

Deadhead

(1) Large floating log, stump, or chunk of flotsam; (2) used as a verb, the positioning voyage of a ship where the vessel is empty. See also **Empty Leg.**

Deadlight

A hinged metal panel that can be secured to the inside of a **porthole** or window to protect the interior of a cabin or other area in the event that heavy seas or other hazards break the glass. In **cruise**

Deadtime Investment Cost

ships, these are generally used for **portholes** located near the waterline and are secured over the glass in rough weather by crew.

Deadtime Investment Cost

The financing cost for a ship, or for a component of a ship, between the time the cost is incurred and the time when the item is actually placed in use and becomes productive.

Deadweight Tonnage

Carrying capacity of a ship expressed in terms of weight. This represents the difference between an empty ship in normal operating condition (with fuel and stores on board) and the same vessel with a full cargo. This term is not usually used in the travel agent/consumer side of the cruise industry, though it still is applied to passenger/cargo ships to describe cargo capacity. For **cruise ships**, it is important in determining refueling cycles.

Death on the High Seas Act (DOHSA)

The Act is triggered by any wrongful act that occurs outside of three nautical miles that results in an individual's death either on sea or on land. It defines legal remedies available for deaths which occur beyond a marine league from U.S. territorial waters. Under DOHSA damages are typically more limited than those available under most state's laws. Under the auspices of this act, U.S. courts have required cruise lines to be accountable via the U.S. legal system even if the cruise line and vessel are foreign. The **Jones Act** of 1920 also provided legal remedies involving the death of seamen.

Debarkation

See **Disembarkation**.

Decision Support System for Masters

SOLAS requires that all ships constructed before July 1, 1997 must have a decision support system for emergency management on the navigation bridge. According to Regulation 24-4.3, "The System shall, as a minimum, consist of a printed emergency plan or plans. The foreseeable emergency situations shall be identified in the emergency plan or plans including, but not limited to, the following main groups of emergencies: fire, damage to ship, pollution, unlawful acts threatening the safety of the ship and the security of its passengers and crew, personnel accidents, cargo-related accidents, and emergency assistance to other ships."

Deck

A level, floor, or story of a vessel.

Deck and Engine

These terms define two of the three major departments and cultures aboard ship (the third, which operates somewhat independently of the other two, is the hotel department). "Deck" denotes the area in charge of navigation, safety, and discipline. Other tasks include the external maintenance of the ship, of navigation equipment, and other responsibilities. The **Captain**, while being in over-all charge of a vessel, directly controls the Deck department, sometimes with the help of another officer such as the **chief officer**. The Engine department, headed by a **chief engineer**, is in charge of the propulsion equipment and, often, other machinery on board such as the air conditioning plant. While rivalry between these two very different groups of people is one of the traditions of the sea, it is important that they work together. Often, officers and crew are of similar nationalities in these two areas to facilitate communication. The phrase "deck and engine" is often used to denote the marine operation of a ship as distinguished from the hotel department.

Deck Hand

A seaman in the Deck Department aboard ship. Seamen undertake a variety of duties at sea or in **port**. These relate to navigation, loading or unloading, as well as maintenance. Examples: anchoring, handling mooring lines, and painting.

Deck Party

Unique to **cruise ships**, such parties are often tied to late-night departures in scenic harbors, and are often themed e.g. Mexican, tropical, 1960's, Reggae, etc.

Deck Plan

Shows layout of **cruise ship** including public rooms, cabins, and decks. The term is usually applied to plans of the hotel portion of the vessel.

More detailed plans that also include engines, crew accommodation, and storage areas are usually called **general arrangement plans**. In the days of classic ships, cabin layouts and fittings varied a great deal, and plans were large enough to illustrate variations with ease. Deck plans were often printed on very thin paper but could be as large as three by five feet. Brochure-sized plans illustrated one deck on each page and frequently included illustrations of cabins and public rooms. Now that cabins are generally standard in size, layout, and fittings, smaller plans suffice – sometimes so small that a magnifying glass is required to read the cabin number.

Deck Steward

A member of the hotel staff assigned to look after passenger needs on deck. This position, on cruise lines where it is still used, is traditionally assigned the function of seeing that deck chairs are clean and properly arranged, and that cushions are in place when needed. In the days of the great liners, certain hotel functions were also undertaken by the deck steward. They ensured that passengers were served tea, coffee, and drinks when desired. Until the 1960's, deck stewards would also make deck chair assignments for passengers, usually in return for a small fee. The names of individuals assigned to specific chairs were inscribed on a paper label in a holder provided for that purpose. This frequently resulted in a far superior standard of deck service than that which is often available today. First, the deck chair was assigned according to individual passenger preference – for shade, sun, whether a view was important, etc. It would be relocated according to time of day and weather conditions. The steward would frequently know the names of those assigned to his section, and would see to their needs on a personal basis. Currently, the functions of deck steward are usually divided between the bar departments (for serving beverages), and the deck crew (for cleaning chairs, putting them in place, and stacking them when needed). One of the last major cruise lines to provide traditional deck steward service was Home Lines.

Deckhead

The underside of a deck; a traditional marine term. In sailing ship days, this was a place one was likely to hit one's head, and was that part of the ship that was overhead.

Deckhouse

Generally used to denote a small structure on deck, which can be square, oblong, or round; frequently used to house an entry to a lower deck or to protect deck equipment. These used to be found frequently on the fore or afterdecks of ships which carried both passengers and cargo. On most modern **cruise ships**, the functions formerly protected by deck houses are incorporated into the main **superstructure** of the vessel.

Decoupling Revenues

Those revenues that contribute to the profitability of a company, as opposed to **passthrough revenues** such as those in payment of airline tickets that do not.

Deed of Convenant

A document that specifies all mortgage conditions associated with a vessel.

Deep Caribbean

Term used in sales and marketing to denote Caribbean cruises that reach islands south and east of St. Maarten. These ports of call are beyond what can be reached on seven-day cruises from South Florida. Therefore, seven-day cruises sailing to the "Deep Caribbean" usually originate in San Juan, but can be based elsewhere e.g. Barbados and Aruba.

Delivery Quay

The **quay** to which a ship is delivered after it has been accepted from the shipyard by the owner. This is generally specified in the contract.

Delivery (Ship)

Delivery of a **cruise ship** occurs when (1) a yard completes construction of a new vessel and it is handed over to its owner for operation; (2) when a company sells a ship and delivers it the buyer; (3) when a ship is handed over to other operators as part of a charter; or (4) when the ship is returned to the owner following completion of the charter, a process also known as **redelivery**. The delivery process requires a detailed protocol including documents attesting to the ownership and operation of the vessel as well as the transfer of responsibility for it from one entity to another. At the time of delivery, inventories and inspections take place as agreed upon by the parties involved. These notably include an accounting of consumable supplies, fuel, lubricant, etc.

Deluxe Cruise Segment

There is little standardization of terminology for market segments above the budget and mass markets. However, many regard such companies as Holland America and Celebrity, as well as some of Princess Cruises, to be in the deluxe segment offering superior cuisine, service, and the more traditional ocean travel amenities, generally in new-ship surroundings. As with all segments, there is some overlap. For instance, some would rate the "Vision" class Royal Caribbean International ships in this category by virtue of their **hardware**, but don't place them there because of the standard mass-market **software**.

Demand Forcasting

The act of determining the total number of bookings likely to be generated for any given sailing whether or not the total demand for the sailing date can be accommodated.

Demise Charter

See **Bare Boat Charter**.

Deployment

Scheduled ship itinerary for a specified period of time. This term is also used to describe the operations of an entire fleet.

Designated Marketing Area (DMA)

Has come to take the place of the traditionally-used term "media market" and refers to an area reachable through advertising via major regional newspapers as well as radio and TV stations.

Designated Person Ashore (DPA)

A person or persons ashore responsible for monitoring safety and pollution control for a ship or ships. This senior company official ensures that adequate resources and shore support are applied as required. The Designated person is part of the **Safety Management System (SMS)** and is required by the **International Safety Management Code (ISM)** adopted by the **IMO**. ISM was made mandatory through its inclusion in the **SOLAS** convention adopted in May, 1994, which took effect on July 1 1998. The provision reflects the increasing control of vessel operation by owners in recent years and is intended to place with them increased responsibility and accountability for safety and anti-pollution measures.

Detention
Prevention from sailing of a vessel found to be in violation of regulations promulgated by the IMO, U.S. Coast Guard, or other state governing authority. Usually, such an act would take place as a result of the Coast Guard's enforcement of IMO directives, perhaps relating to **SOLAS**.

Destination Cruises
Cruises where the prime attraction is the destination(s) rather than the shipboard experience.

Det Norske Veritas (DNV)
Norwegian **classification society**.

Deviation Desk
Department established by many cruise lines to administer special passenger requests concerning air transportation to and from the ship. In upscale lines, this can be an art and can involve such items as chartering a private jet. Normally, the Desk deals with such matters as upgrades and changes in schedule, route, or class.

Diarrhea Count
See **Mr. "D" Count**.

Diesel Assisted Sailing Vessel
A ship primarily dependent on sails for propulsion, but with diesel capability in order to maintain a fixed schedule. This is in contrast to **sail assisted cruise ships** where engines are the prime motive power and sails are provided largely for aesthetic reasons. The major company building diesel-assisted sailing vessels is Star Clipper Cruises. Here, the ship is primarily a sailing vessel. The best

example of the concept of "sail-assisted" is Windstar. Both types spend as much time as practical under sail; the difference is in basic ship design.

Diesel electric propulsion system

The prime motive power of most **cruise ships** currently being built, this involves the use of diesel engines to generate electricity which, in turn, drive the primary electric propulsion motor. This mode of propulsion is quieter and more flexible than **direct drive** diesels, and there is less vibration. Machinery is commonly mounted on rafts that are, in turn, flexibly mounted on the ship's **hull**. This technology does not require gearing, and enables a ship to operate with maximum efficiency at any speed. This method of propelling a ship is also efficient because main engines can be used to generate optimally the great amounts of electricity that all **cruise ships** require. This obviates the need to have separate electricity generators.

Dilution

(1) Extent to which **theoretical revenue** is reduced when actual revenue is computed; (2) dilution in earnings per share caused by issuance of new shares.

Direct Business

Cruise bookings made directly with the cruise line by the consumer. Once rare, the Internet has made this more of a factor in the general profile of cruise line sales in North America. In the United States, agents still book 98% of cruises. In Europe, direct business is more common. When a line sells cruises through a travel agency that it owns, the issue of what constitutes "direct business" becomes a little blurred. There may be an increase in North American direct business as Carnival and Renaissance turn to the Internet as a source of additional passengers and revenue.

Direct Drive Diesels

Configuration for low-speed diesel engines serving as main propulsion units driving the propeller without a gearbox. Where a medium-speed engine is used, the difference between engine speed and propeller revolutions is accommodated by gearing.

Diesel electric propulsion has replaced geared diesels as the prime **cruise ship** main engine system. It is even more flexible and normally provides less vibration.

Disabled, Cabin for

Cabins designed to accommodate disabled passengers. **SOLAS** guidelines adopted several years ago provide guidance on designing for the elderly and disabled passenger. New vessels have increasingly been designed to accommodate the needs of the physically challenged guest.

Disembarkation

The act of leaving a ship.

Displacement Tonnage

The amount of water displaced by the vessel, or the actual weight of the ship. This measure is not often used to describe **cruise ships,** but is meaningful in describing military vessels. It was often used in defining treaty limitations when applied to a given type of warship. Thirty-five cubic feet of seawater are displaced for each ton of vessel weight. Displacement tonnage is applied to a ship in normal operating state i.e. with fuel and stores on board. It frequently is used as a means of establishing canal tolls and fees.

Disposed

Word traditionally used in the shipping industry in connection with the sale of a ship. It has a slightly negative connotation and is used more often when a ship is sold for scrapping, when the standards it represents are well below the rest of the seller's fleet, or if a cruise line is being reduced because of negative circumstances, e.g. financial exigency. If a ship merely changes hands and both buyer and seller are strong, the word "sold" is more often used. Because of its negative connotation, this word is generally avoided by the principals in any sale.

Distant Foreign Port

In order to carry passengers between two U.S. ports, a **cruise ship** must call at a "distant foreign port." The legal definition of this is "…any foreign port that is not a **nearby foreign port.**" For a list of areas where the seaports are excluded from status as "distant foreign port," see **Nearby Foreign Port**.

Distillation Plant
Converts salt water to fresh water aboard ship. The process is known as desalination, reverse osmosis, or R.O.

Distress Signal (Mayday)
Taken from the French expression, "M'Aidez," this consists of an internationally recognized radiotelegraph or radiotelephone transmission indicating grave or imminent danger and requesting immediate assistance. If the signal is transmitted by radiotelegraph, the signal consists of three dots, three dashes, and three dots transmitted as a single signal. If the signal is sent via radiotelephone, it consists of the enunciation of the word "Mayday", which is the anglisized version of "M'Aidez" or "Help me."

District Sales Manager (DSM)
Generic term for the manager in charge of sales within a specific geographic area. In fact, individual cruise lines have now coined company-specific terms for this position, for example Business Development Manager at Carnival.

DOC
See **Document of Compliance.**

Dock
(1) Usually used to refer to a harbor-side construct where a ship, or tenders from a ship, tie up to load or unload passengers and/or supplies; literally means the water occupied by the ship when moored rather than the structure/pier itself; (2) used as a verb, to arrive ("to dock").

Dockage
A fee levied by port authorities for the right to **dock** a vessel. The basis for dockage varies from **port** to port and may include such items as length, tonnage, passenger capacity, duration of stay (sometimes in hours) – one, two, or several factors.

Document of Compliance (DOC)

Issued to a company that complies with the requirements of the **International Safety Management Code (ISM)**. This document is issued by the country in which the ship is registered. After a shipowner receives its DOC, each ship in the line is individually inspected to receive a Safety Management Certificate. Each of these certificates is valid for up to five years.

DOHSA

See **Death on High Seas Act.**

Dolphin

A permanent islet built of wood, stone, or concrete used to moor a vessel. There are two types of dolphins: a mooring dolphin is used to tie up a ship; a breasting dolphin is used to keep a ship from rubbing against a dock.

Double Bottom

Heavily compartmentalized area at the bottom of a ship. In the event that the outer bottom is holed, the inner hull will maintain the watertight integrity of the vessel. The void between inner and outer hulls is frequently used for seawater **ballast** or for fuel. Voids can also be useful for maintaining **stability** when a vessel is damaged.

Double Occupancy (as Fare and Capacity Basis)

The standard unit for quoting cruise fares and, generally, for computing a ship's capacity. This is in contrast with hotels where most (though not all) quote rates for a room rather than per person, and where capacity measurement is usually expressed in number of rooms rather than number of beds.

Downgrade

To assign a passenger accommodation in a lower cabin category than originally purchased. This is rare. **Upgrades**, used as a marketing tool, have become common.

Draft

The depth of water required by a vessel to float; the measurement in feet or meters of the extent to which a ship projects below the surface of the water. This normally refers to a **cruise ship** in stan-

Draft Limits

dard operating condition with stores and fuel embarked. **SOLAS** defines it as the distance between the **subdivision load line** and the "moulded base line" or bottom of the ship. Along with such factors as length and beam, draft is important in determining the ports at which a ship may safely dock or anchor. An important advance in modern **cruise ship** design is the limited draft of even the largest modern **cruise ship**. The great liners of the 1930's drew well in excess of thirty feet. Dual purpose classic liners intended for cruising and transoceanic service typically drew 28.5 feet. Most modern **cruise ships** draw about twenty-five feet which means that typically length becomes a more important consideration than draft when choosing ports. The terms "light draft" and "load draft" apply to the draft of cargo ships or combivessels with and without cargo.

Draft Limits

The maximum draft allowed for a **cruise ship** or other vessel to enter a harbor or transit a canal.

Drag

(1) State of increased resistance to passage through the water. Causes of drag can be a damaged **hull**; **stabilizers** extended and in operation; the condition of being out of **trim**; a hull with marine growth; absence of optimum design of rudder or **propeller**; or abnormally deep **draft**; or (2) when the **anchor** does not grab hold of the ocean or harbor bottom and, by being dragged, fails to hold the ship in a stationary position.

Draught

See **Draft**.

Dress Ship

Hanging flags or pennants from lines to and from **masts** to decorate a ship on a special occasion such as a **maiden voyage**, a holiday, or on any other occasion when this is desired. Since **cruise ships** no longer have traditional masts fore and aft, the lines are frequently rigged from the **bow** to the radar mast and aft to the vessel's **funnel** and **stern**. Lights are often hung on these same lines for decorative purposes.

Dry Dock

Drive Market

The market that is within driving range of a port where a vessel is based. Typically, this means about four hours of driving time in North America. Europeans, however, frequently drive from six to ten hours with the incentive to sail the Mediterranean. Varies from market to market in view of consumer options available.

Dropped Option

(1) When a cruise line orders a ship, the company often places an option for a second or third similar vessel in order to lock in price and delivery date. A dropped option occurs when that option is not exercised. Sometimes, that option will then be purchased by another company. An example of this is the purchase of *Royal Viking Queen* when the option was dropped by Seabourn (the ship was eventually repurchased by Seabourn and sails as the *Seabourn Legend*); (2) when a passenger makes a reservation for a cruise, he or she is given an option for the space that must be confirmed by payment of a deposit. If an individual does not make such a payment, or decides not to book, the result is a dropped option.

Dry Dock

(1) An enclosed basin in a shipyard that, when pumped dry, makes it possible to do work on the underwater portion of a **cruise ship**; floating drydocks can be partially submerged to accept a ship, then are pumped dry when the ship has entered the facility; (2) used as a generic term for a vessel's maintenance period when a ship actually enters a drydock. To maintain **class**, modern **cruise ships** are usually required to undergo drydocking twice every five years. In the days of the great liners, all passenger ships had to be drydocked at least annually to remove marine growth from the bottom – sometimes more often. This is now rendered unnecessary by modern **hull** finishes and periodic underwater maintenance by divers. Periodic drydock work is necessary for refinishing the underwater hull and for maintaining **rudders**, **stabilizers, propeller** shafts (also known as **tail shafts**), and paint. Failure to maintain a ship's

underwater hull can result in loss of speed and/or increased fuel consumption. See also **wet dock**, when a ship's maintenance period does not involve actually entering a drydock.

E

Early Booking Discount (EBD)

In order to encourage passengers to book early, lines started to offer discounts for early bookings in the 1980's. The cost to companies of such discounts is partially or completely recouped through interest earned on the deposit. The EBD is used by some lines to solve cash flow problems, but primarily it is a tool to help ensure that when a ship sails, all cabins are full.

Earnings Per Share (EPS)

All publicly-traded companies must disclose their basic earnings for each outstanding common share and diluted earnings for each outstanding common share and other potentially diluted securities.

Eastern Caribbean, Cruises to

One of the most popular itineraries for week-long **mass market** cruises that originate in South Florida, these sailings typically depart Fort Lauderdale and Miami and include calls at San Juan, St. Thomas, St. Maarten, and sometimes an **out island** beach party stop and/or Nassau. The first seven-day cruises in the modern cruise industry sailed to the Eastern Caribbean. Today, this itinerary appeals to those who like time at sea and find the scenic attractions of these destinations desirable.

EBD

See Early Booking Discount.

Embarkation

The process of passengers and/or **crew** going aboard a vessel for the first time during the initial day of the cruise. Not normally used to denote the process of returning on board at ports of call. Final departure from the ship on the last day of the voyage is referred to as disembarkation.

Embarkation Agent

The individual responsible for embarking (and, usually, disembarking) passengers either in the home port or at a port remote from the starting point of the cruise. The agent reviews tickets, issues boarding passes, and checks other applicable travel documents. Sometimes this process is done aboard ship by the vessel's own staff. Usually, the agent is a cruise line employee, at times the line's agent, and at times employed by a subcontractor providing services to the cruise line.

Embarkation Lunch

Frequently, **cruise ships** are available for boarding at noon or shortly thereafter on the day of sailing. It is customary to provide a light lunch for early-boarding passengers, food service that may well extend to the middle of the afternoon. This is especially useful when arrival of **air-sea** passengers creates a spread of passenger boarding times.

Emergency Condition

SOLAS term for the situation where services needed for **normal operational and habitable conditions** are not functioning due to the loss of electrical power.

Emergency Response System (ERS)

Codified procedure for handling oil pollution emergencies; involves both shoreside and shipboard segments. This is required by **MARPOL** and by some government agencies. Involves reporting to appropriate agencies, such as the Coast Guard, emergencies while they are taking place. ERS provides the basis for coordinated response to an emergency at sea. Under the newly enacted International Safety Management Code, an ERS will be part of an established Safety Management System.

Emergency Steering Room (or Station)

Location where the vessel may be steered manually in the event of power failure, catastrophic accident, etc.

Empty Leg

To undertake a positioning voyage (where the objective is to get a ship to a destination, rather than to make money) with the ship empty of passengers. These are rare, since with coordinated charter flights, it is possible to book almost any voyage anywhere. Land arrangements can be included where appropriate. At times, cruise lines will **deadhead** a ship en route to a shipyard where a refit is to be undertaken. Free of passengers, the work can begin during the transfer voyage. **Cruise ships** often sail empty to do charter work. **Cabotage** laws at times prevent the booking of passengers during a positioning voyage. The term is sometimes used for a block of cabins that may be vacant for part of a cruise in order to accommodate passengers during a later segment.

Engineers' Alarm

An alarm activated from a ship's control room or the maneuvering platform that is plainly audible in the engineers' accommodation.

EPS

See **Earnings Per Share**.

Ergonomics

Applied to the cruise industry, providing equipment and surroundings that both meet regulatory requirements and the needs of those working with them.

ERS

See **Emergency Response System**.

Estimated Time of Arrival.

The time a vessel is expected to arrive at a port, pilot station, to begin a canal transit, etc.

Estimated Time of Availability

The time a ship is expected to be available – following shipyard refit, charter, sale, etc.

ETA

See **Estimated Time of Arrival** and **Estimated Time of Availability**.

Even Keel

When a ship is in **trim** i.e. draws the same amount of water fore and aft. The term is commonly misused to denote an absence of **list**.

Expedition Vessels
Small **cruise ships** for passengers interested in visiting remote parts of the world or ports off the beaten path. These are frequently reinforced for navigation in ice, and enable passengers to get close to natural wonders, fauna, and flora. Two prime cruising areas for expedition vessels are Alaska and Antarctica. These are also used to visit the Galapagos Islands. Fares are usually quite high due to the limited number of passengers that can be accommodated and, often, the number of staff required to support this style of cruising. Additional personnel are sometimes needed to transport passengers ashore in **wet landings**, to provide specialist lectures, and to embrace the high number of crew per passenger entailed in the operation of a small ship. Expedition passengers are part of what is known as **niche** cruising.

Experienced Cruisers
As used in cruise demographics, anyone who has cruised before but not with the same company. In more general usage on the consumer side, the term usually refers to those who have taken four, five, or more cruises.

Extreme Draft
Draft at its greatest (deepest) point; also known as keel draft.

Eyes of the Ship
Openings where the **hawsepipe** pierces the **hull** forward, allowing for the passage of the **anchor** chain with anchor attached. Viewed from ahead, these openings have the appearance of eyes. The term is usually used to denote the area of the ship where the "eyes" are located.

F

Facilitation of International Maritime Traffic (FAL)
FAL provides uniformity in arrival, stay, and departure procedures for vessels entering and leaving ports. The convention, organized by the **IMO**, came into force in 1997.

Factor of Subdivision

SOLAS prescribes the way to determine the maximum length allowable between watertight **bulkheads**. This is determined by multiplying the **floodable length** by the **factor of subdivision**. The convention includes the formula for determining the latter.

Fair Wind

A following wind that increases, rather than decreases, the speed of the ship. With modern **cruise ships,** and their large **sail area**, whether the wind is a headwind or a following wind can make a difference in the progress of a voyage.

Fairway

Deep area, or channel, outside the harbor entrance.

FAL

See **Facilitation of International Maritime Traffic.**

Fall Foliage Cruises

Cruises offered during the late summer and early fall to Canada and New England. Although the season is limited to about two months and requires redeployment of vessels from other areas, these cruises are very profitable and popular in spite of the uncertain weather. Cruise lines in search of new cruising areas for repeat passengers are tending to commence the Canada/New England cruise season in midsummer, something permitted by the availability of new ships. Variations in itinerary include one-way cruises between New York/Boston and Montreal/Quebec City; five- or seven-day round-trips from New York or Boston stopping short of the St. Lawrence; and sailings of ten days or longer round-trip from New York that permit itineraries to include Quebec City and a variety of other destinations.

Fam Trip

A reduced-rate cruise provided for a group of travel agents to familiarize them with the product. Such trips include seminars for participants as well as unstructured time.

Family Cabin

Rooms that can accommodate five or more passengers in permanent berths. Standard cabins are often able to accommodate up to four passengers in permanent berths (two lower and two upper). However, in recent years family cruising has increased and with it, provision of cabins specifically designed for families. The Disney ships have a number of cabins that can accommodate up to six passengers. See also **cabin**. Relatively new developments are features intended to make cabin occupancy by four or five individuals more comfortable. These include two washrooms and sliding privacy panels.

FAS

See **Free Alongside**.

Fast Ferry

A recent generation of ferries that cruise at speeds of 25 **knots** or more. These generally have overnight accommodation, carry cars, and can resemble **cruise ships**. A feature of them is extensive provision for duty-free shopping.

Fathom

International nautical measure equal to 1.8256 meters or about six feet.

FCCA

See **Florida Caribbean Cruise Association**.

Federal Maritime Commission Bond (FMC Bond)

Protects the deposits and passage money paid by passengers for cruises originating in the United States and not yet taken – this in the event a company becomes insolvent. Current protection required is a maximum of $15 million. Federal legislation was first enacted in 1966 following several bankruptcies by marginal operators. Initial protection followed the collapse of Caribbean Cruise Lines in 1964, an event that stranded passengers in several **ports** and resulted in lost ticket money. Prior to the bankruptcy, there had been operational problems with chartered ships that became the subject of congressional hearings. The Caribbean Cruise Lines event had followed the insolvency of the Swiss-owned Arosa Line in 1958. The collapse of Regency Cruises in 1996 called into question the adequacy of protection of current bonding levels since there was substantial loss of

Federal Maritime Commission (FMC)

passage money including funds paid in advance for a world cruise. As this is written, FMC is reviewing a proposal to increase the bonding levels required of vessel operators.

Federal Maritime Commission (FMC)

An independent agency composed of five commissioners, including a chairman, who are appointed by the President with the advice and consent of the Senate. The FMC regulates marine traffic to and from the United States. It exercises a protective function in relation to the practices of foreign-flag carriers; investigates related complaints; sees that a competitive environment is maintained; maintains tariff filings including rates, rules, and charges of carriers; licenses freight forwarders based in U.S.; requires cruise industry bonds (see **Federal Maritime Commission Bond**); and certifies financial responsibility of cruise lines and other carriers. In cruise-line-related matters, it has no jurisdiction over vessel operations, navigation, seafaring personnel, or navigation aids.

Federal Prevention of Pollution from Ships Act

Prohibits the discharge of untreated bilge water within three miles of the U.S. coastline. Reflecting **MARPOL** agreements, there are also numerous other restrictions such as those against the dumping of glass, plastics, oil, and food.

Ferry

This term is usually applied to a vessel transporting passengers and vehicles from point to point, but is also used in connection with ships transporting only vehicles and their drivers. The ferry industry is highly developed in the Mediterranean and the Baltic and, especially in the latter area, is patronized by passengers in search of duty-free shopping. This industry overlaps the cruise industry. Indeed, early modern **cruise ships** built in the late Sixties and early Seventies drew on shipbuilding technology and generic designs developed for the ferry industry. The early **cruise ships** that resulted were high density, featured small cabins (122 square feet was typical), and, as with NCL's *Starward*, carried both trucks and cruise passengers in early years of service. Later, garage spaces became cabins. The European ferry industry continues to yield design concepts that are occasionally copied in **cruise ship** plans. One example is the forward multi-level lounge of *CostaVictoria*, inspired by the fast, modern ferries of the Silja Line and other Baltic ferries. The typical ferry passenger is going from point to point and spends only a short time aboard ship. Even when sailings are sold as round-trip mini-cruises, the time spent aboard is limited. These ships can therefore carry a large number of passengers for their size. Usually, passage is available both in cabins or in airliner-style reclining seats. Generally, meals are not included in the price of the passage ticket.

Final Leg

The last segment of a cruise – between the final **port** of call and arrival at the terminal port where passengers will **disembark**. Has come into frequent usage because of the number of vital tasks that must be completed during this time.

Final Sailing

The ship has not only left the pier, but has also reached the entrance to the port and is proceeding. In commercial terms, the ship has sailed. Of course, this can also refer to the last voyage in a given season, on a particular service, or the final sailing for all time.

FIO

See **Free In and Out.**

Fire Doors

This generic term is usually applied to doors built to a standard that supports the division of the ship into main vertical zones and which meet the standard of **"A Class"** divisions. As prescribed in the **SOLAS** standards, they are constructed of steel or other equivalent material and meet very high standards retarding heat and flame.

Fire Patrol

Required by **SOLAS**, Chapter II-2, for ships carrying more than thirty-six passengers. Training requirements for the patrol are specified, including familiarity with the ship and with fire equipment.

Fire Rating

An international measure of the ability of a **bulk-**

head or door to resist or retard fire. This rating is measured with a letter and number combination e.g. B15, which is the required rating for many doors aboard a **cruise ship**. B15 indicates, among other requirements, that the panel will have an insulation value such that the average temperature on the unexposed side will not rise more than 139C above the original temperature for a period of fifteen minutes, and will not exceed 225C at any point. The international **SOLAS** laws specify in detail the fire ratings required throughout a ship.

Fire Sale

A sometimes desperate effort to sell cruise cabins when a substantial number of them remain unsold shortly before a sailing date. "Fire sales" are used in cases where a ship has an unexpected number of cancellations on short notice; where a charter or part-charter is cancelled; when a line's projections regarding berths sold prove to be inaccurate, perhaps due to a downturn in the economy, or an act of war that has taken place in the region of the itinerary; bad publicity affecting the line; or for other reasons. "Fire sales" are not very common in the North American market as this tends to be stable and predictable when times are good. However, they are more common in Europe where vessels come in and out of charters on very short notice and cabins are sometimes released in large numbers by tour operators without major advance warning. In such cases, extensive discounts of as much as 80% are offered through agents and tour operators. The rationale is that an unsold cabin loses not only the basic fare but also the on board revenue that is generated by the occupants.

First Seating

See **Seatings, Late and Early.**

First Time Cruisers

A majority of passengers in the mass-market segment of the cruise industry, and 44% over-all, are first-timers. Since satisfaction with the experience and value occurs in most cases, many first-time cruisers become repeaters. Thus, this group represents an important element in the future of the industry. Attracting first-timers is the cornerstone of marketing efforts by such companies as Carnival, NCL, and Royal Caribbean.

Fixed Costs

Costs that continue regardless of the level of activity in an organization or ship. There are several different categories of fixed costs. There are those, such as depreciation and the cost of shoreside headquarters, that continue even when no ship is operating. At sea, there are fixed costs that continue in an operating ship regardless of the number of passengers on board. Examples of these are deck and engine crew, officers, and fuel. Ashore there are fixed costs that continue regardless of number of passengers being booked, and transaction-related costs that vary with level of activity. At Carnival Cruise Lines, there is accounting (fixed cost) and revenue accounting (variable, according to number of ships and passengers being booked). The trend toward megaships is, in part, due to the tendency of fixed costs not to increase proportionately with number of passengers accommodated. As a fleet increases in size, shoreside fixed costs usually do not increase proportionately.

Flag Administration

See **Administration**.

Flag of Convenience

A **country of registry** or flag **administration** that does not necessarily reflect either the ownership or home base of a cruise line but which is adopted to minimize taxes, operating costs, and restrictions to operations such as staffing practices.

Flagship

The largest or the most prestigious vessel in the fleet of a cruise line. Where the official practice exists of having a Commodore, or senior captain, the vessel where he is stationed is considered the flagship. The institution of having a flagship and a Commodore is now mainly practiced by the British, as exemplified by Princess and P & O. In other lines and nationalities, the distinction has fallen into disuse. Generically, however, the term "flagship" is still used by laymen applicable to the company's largest or most prestigious **cruise ship** even if, officially, no flagship exists. The official

Flat Commission

practice gets in the way of flexibility in assignment and related coordination of leaves, retirements, and the need for a particular expertise in a captain in a given vessel or service.

Flat Commission

Where a travel agent commission is based on a fixed sum of money or fixed percentage rather than a graduated scale. This is generally frowned upon by the travel industry as limiting income. In a flat commission situation, there are no **overrides** and, hence, no special incentives for volume sales.

Fleet

Two or more vessels in a cruise line; also used to refer to the **cruise ships** serving a given area, a market, or the entire industry. When Ted Arison was organizing Carnival Cruise Lines, he expected to purchase Cunard's *Carmania* and *Franconia* rather than the single ship *Empress of Canada*, renamed *Mardi Gras*, with which he founded the line. Thus, Carnival was originally advertised as the "Golden Fleet" even though it initially consisted of only one ship.

Floating Dry Dock

The most commonly-built form of **drydock** today, the drydock walls and floor have compartments that may be flooded to lower the dock and permit the entry of a vessel. When the ship is properly positioned, the interior of the dock is pumped dry and work on the outer hull of the vessel can begin. Floating on the surface of the water, these can be a dramatic site with the bow or stern of a ship fully exposed. See also **dry dock** and **graving dock**.

Floating Resort

Effectively, the definition of a modern **cruise ship**. Variations of this are the "Floating Villages" of Club Med when they decided to go into the cruise business with Club *Med I* and *II*. The former is now the *Windsurf*, sailing for Windstar.

Floodable Length

Term used in **SOLAS** meaning the length of a vessel below the **bulkhead deck** that can be flooded "…without the ship being submerged beyond the **margin line**. In the absence of a continuous bulkhead deck, the water must reach no higher than 76mm below "...the top of the deck (at side) to which the bulkheads concerned and the shell are carried watertight. Factors that influence floodable length include form, draft, and other design factors.

Florida Caribbean Cruise Association

Established by the cruise industry to further good working relationships with governments and ports in the Caribbean, and to deal with a number of operational issues relating to cruise operations in the area. Founded in 1972 by John Weber, Executive Vice President of what was then Norwegian Caribbean Lines. Up until that time, relationships with the area had been handled by the North Atlantic Passenger Association since most vessels cruising the area were Atlantic liners owned by North Atlantic operators. Because these lines were primarily European owned, most meetings were held in Europe. Emerging cruise companies at that time – NCL, Commodore, Eastern, and Costa – tended not to have their interests adequately represented.

Flotsam and Jetsam

Flotsam represents goods or equipment thrown overboard because of spoilage or to lighten a ship in an emergency; jetsam, items thrown overboard for any reason.

Fly Acts

Entertainment cabaret acts engaged for a series of performances on more than one ship. Typically, they will begin a cruise on one ship, then leave the ship and fly to another at a port of call. Thus, an entertainer may perform on two or three ships within a seven-day period.

Fly-Cruise

A cruise sold inclusive of air-transportation and, usually, transfers between ship and airport. This is the basis on which most cruises are sold today. The fly-cruise made it possible to begin winter cruises in warm-water ports, eliminating a two-day passage through winter seas and enormously increasing the appeal of a cruise. Typical winter cruise departure ports in the 1950's were Southampton, England

and New York. Currently, most departures are from South Florida, San Juan, and, for the European market, these and other West Indies ports. The shift to fly-cruising began on a small scale in the 1960's and gained momentum in the 1970's.

FMC
See **Federal Maritime Commission**.

FMC Bond
See **Federal Maritime Commission Bond**.

FO
See **Free Out**.

Following Sea
Situation where the waves, and most likely the wind, move in the direction the ship is sailing. This creates the most comfortable motion appreciated by crew and passengers alike. However, in the tropics, to the extent that the speed of the ship is the same as that of the wind, it can be hot. Under some circumstances, such conditions can seriously affect a ship's stability.

Food and Bar Manager
Hotel officer responsible for cuisine and bar service and product.

Food Transport Area
Space through which food is transported before, during, or after preparation. Some preparation is handled in compartments adjacent to cold storage spaces deep in the ship before being transported to kitchens for final cooking or other preparation. For instance, by the time vegetables arrive in the galley, they have been peeled and cleaned. Like many other sections of a ship, the food transport area is subject to U.S. Public Health Service inspection.

Force Majeure
The clause in a contract that exempts parties from fulfiling obligations under it in the event of such contingencies as earthquakes, war, floods, or other items beyond their control.

Forced Overnight
The practice of flying in passengers on transcontinental flights overnight, with an early morning arrival when it is not possible to schedule daytime flights prior to a late-afternoon sailing. At such

times, hotel rooms are provided on arrival for passengers to recover from the rigors of red-eye travel. Forced over-nights are usually necessary for passengers on cruises from South Florida who begin their air journey to the ship on the West Coast of North America.

Fore

Forward of **amidships**; toward the **bow** of a vessel.

Forecastle (Fo'c'sle)

Top portion of the **bow**. In the days of line voyage ships, this area was often separated from the main **superstructure** by a drop of one **deck** level forming an area called the **well deck**. This tended to break up waves coming over the bow, thus protecting the superstructure. The *Queen Mary* and many other liners had this feature. It was eliminated on the first *Queen Elizabeth* to provide more space and to create a more streamlined appearance. In smaller, older ships, this area was where **crew** were housed, though generally on passenger ships this was used for general storage purposes with staff housed elsewhere. The term forecastle stems from renaissance sailing ships which had tower-like structures resembling castles at bow and **stern** – hence forecastle. The term has fallen into disuse since, in contemporary marine architecture with the advance of **cruise ship** superstructures almost to the bow, the structural feature of the forecastle has ceased to be a distinctive element of passenger ship design.

Forecastle Head

Open deck atop the **bow**, over the **forecastle**. Since few **cruise ships** actually have forecastles, the term has fallen into disuse.

Forgone Tips

Gratuities paid to service **crew** (tipping-category employees on a vessel with conventional **tipping policies**) where they are deprived of tips through circumstances beyond their control. Example: a ship is damaged and out of service for a period.

Formal Dress

Formal Dress
When used as a recommended style of dress for an evening aboard ship, usually means either a tuxedo or dark suit for men (on casual cruises, jacket and tie) and cocktail dress or evening gown for women.

Formal Evening
Aboard ship, "formal" is interpreted to mean either a dark suit or tuxedo for men, and cocktail dresses or gowns for women. On three- and four-day cruises from South Florida, few don truly formal wear though for longer cruises the pattern is more mixed. Not surprisingly, the number dressing in tuxedos and gowns is usually in direct proportion to the cost of the cruise. Aboard Seabourn and Silversea, formal attire is taken for granted on such evenings.

Forum non conveniens
A legal doctrine under which a court may decline jurisdiction on the grounds the subject matter of a suit, its parties and potential witnesses bear little relationship to the forum court. Under these circumstances, justice is better served by a trial in a more convenient locale. This facilitates litigation by passengers where a ship may be registered under a foreign flag, where the incident may have taken place in a foreign country, or where the ship is owned abroad.

Forward
Toward the **bow** of a ship. Usually refers to an area on the ship, rather than to one ahead of it.

Foul Ground
Area in which to avoid **anchoring**, if possible, because obstructions are likely to damage the anchor.

Fouled Propeller
The presence of a rope, fishline, cable, or other debris tangled in a **propeller**. This is a common marine hazard that can cause damage not only to propellers but to schedules.

Founder
To sink – an older term no longer used frequently. Not to be confused with flounder, the fish.

Free Alongside
A term of sale wherein the seller of goods is

responsible for delivering them to the pier in a position where they can be loaded by the ship's own gear.

Free Height
The height of a cabin or public space available to the passenger, and to the interior designer in planning furniture and other amenities. It is the height to the **deckhead** less the space required by air conditioning ducts, lighting, and other utilities, usually obscured by a false ceiling. This is specified in shipyard contracts.

Free In and Out (FIO)
A term of sale or of a contract of carriage whereby the shipper absorbs the cost of loading or unloading a vessel. Usually used in the freight shipping industry. The shipper may also be the charterer of the ship.

Free on Board (FOB)
A term of sale or of a contract of carriage whereby the shipper undertakes to load the cargo.

Free Out
Cost of unloading a ship is the responsibility of the shipper (who may also be the charterer).

Free Port
See **Foreign Trade Zone**.

Free Trade Zone
An area or port designated by a country where non-prohibited duty-free goods may be stored, displayed, or used, and then re-exported without duty. Also known as a free port.

Freeboard
That part of a ship's **hull** above the waterline.

Freighter Cruises
Passage aboard a freighter with twelve or fewer passengers. In days of **break bulk** freight ships, the vessels would frequently stay in **port** for extended periods of time affording the opportunity to see areas of the world in depth. Fares then were also very modest. In the container age, port calls are sometimes limited to a few hours, frequently in the middle of the night. Fares commonly are in the $100 per day per-person double range. Schedules are only slightly more predictable than they were

prior to containerships. In the opinion of many, the **cruise ship** offers a more competitive value, though containerships still have their appeal thanks to the informal life style they embrace. See also **combivessel**, a cargo ship carrying more than twelve passengers and with a much more varied range of facilities.

Fresh Water Conditions

A vessel will have a deeper draft in fresh water, a factor to be taken into consideration in planning cruise programs.

Fresh Water Production

See **Distillation Plant**.

Full Rudder

When the rudder is turned to **port** or **starboard** in order to create the maximum rate of turn in a vessel.

Full-ship Charter

See **Charter**.

Funnel

Structure that houses exhaust pipes for a **cruise ship's** diesel engines at the top of the ship; or, in the case of a steamship, provides for dispersion of boiler smoke through pipes from the engine room to the top or sides of the funnel structure. A major design challenge for modern **cruise ships,** which burn inexpensive grades of diesel fuel, is to disperse soot away from passenger decks regardless of speed or wind condition and direction. This may well be one of the most common points of failure in modern **cruise ship** design. It is important to project the exhaust to a point outside the stream of air that passes over the ship so that waste products of combustion are not drawn down onto the ship. Wind tunnel tests are helpful, but by no means guarantee a successful outcome. Prior to World War I, passenger ships commonly had false or dummy funnels since these tended to enhance the impression of size and speed in a ship. This could be a helpful marketing tool in advertising the ship to immigrants an important source of revenue. Thus, such ships as *Olympic* and *Titanic* had one dummy funnel each for this purpose and to balance the profile. Since funnels remain one of the most important visual features of a ship's exterior, passenger ships in more modern times have had dummy funnels to balance profiles and improve external appearance. Examples: the *America* of United States Lines, and most of the postwar passenger and **cruise ships** of the Swedish American Line. Two patented funnel features in modern **cruise ships:** Carnival Cruise Lines wing-like funnel structures, and Royal Caribbean International's funnels with Viking Crown Lounges. Another new vessel, the *Rotterdam VI* of Holland America Line, adopted twin funnel pipe-style uptakes as a tribute to *Rotterdam V*. The Disney ships have a dummy forefunnel to balance the profile and make the vessels resemble classic passenger liners. Indeed, the last major passenger ship built with two funnels arranged fore- and aft on the centerline was the 1966 *Kungsholm* of Swedish American Line, now sailing as P & O's *Victoria*. To make the ship look different, the new owners removed the forefunnel and replaced the aft one with a unit considered to be more modern – much to the detriment of the ship's appearance.

G

GA Plan

See **General Arrangement Plans**.

Gale

Wind that measures force eight and nine on the **Beaufort Scale** with a velocity of between thirty-four and forty-seven **knots**. In this sea state, waves are high and crests tend to disintegrate into spray or **spindrift**.

Galley

A kitchen on a ship. On a modern **cruise ship**, there may be several galleys equipped to handle the dietary needs of several **crew** nationalities and religions. Also, several dining rooms on very large ships may have individual galleys.

Gang

Team of longshoremen.

Gangplank
See **Gangway**.

Gangway
Narrow walkway used by passengers and **crew** to board a ship. In most **ports**, there will generally be a separate gangway for crew. In a modern cruise terminal, the gangway resembles a jetway used to board aircraft. In the days of ocean **liners**, there would usually be separate gangways for each class of passengers in addition to one for crew. See also **Passenger Boarding Bridges** and **Accommodation Ladder**.

Gas Turbine
Developed by GE Marine as a new power source for **cruise ships,** the system is already in use aboard naval vessels. A jet turbine, the design offers advantages in space utilization and in other areas. First major cruise line to use the system is Royal Caribbean in the "Voyager" and "Millennium" ships. A drawback, from the cost standpoint, is that fuel used is more expensive than that required by diesel vessels. Advantages include the ability to steam at high speeds at lower cost, assuming stability in the price of fuel; smaller engine size making possible the use of space saved for revenue purposes; and lighter weight. Technical name: "Combined Gas Turbine and Steam Turbine Integrated Electric Drive." Not really new, it has been used for years in military ships.

Gateway
(1) City where the cruise passenger boards an aircraft and begins the journey to the **port** where **embarkation** on a **cruise ship** will take place; (2) port city used by **cruise ships** that is an entry point for a country or region. The term is used variously in other segments of the travel industry.

Gay and Lesbian Cruise
The gay segment of the cruise industry is a growing one. The label is applied either for charters or group bookings. One of the best-known gay travel organizations is RSVP. Two others are Atlantis, and Olivia which organizes Lesbian groups and charters. RSVP pioneered the gay cruise charter and, for a time, owned its own small **cruise ship**. Special

staff orientation is often undertaken to ensure that service standards are maintained. Special entertainment features afloat and ashore are usually part of the package.

GCD (Guest Cruise Day)
See **Passenger Cruise Day**.

General Arrangements Plan
A **deck** plan showing the layout of each deck including mechanical, crew spaces, and even the double bottom.

General Average (G.A.)
In the marine world, "average" means loss or damage. Frequently referred to as "G.A.", in the event of loss or damage to a vessel, all parties who have invested in the voyage share the loss based on their respective stakes. This becomes especially important when a vessel is operating under a **charter** agreement. The procedure dates back to the Rhodian Sea Codes of Ancient Greece.

General Emergency Alarm
Seven or more short blasts followed by one long blast on the ship's whistle or siren "…and additionally on an electrically operated bell or klaxon or other equivalent warning system, which shall be powered from the ship's main supply and the emergency source of electrical power…" (**SOLAS**).

General Sales Agent
Acts as sales and marketing representative for a cruise line in a specific country where the line desires a foreign-market presence. Provides liaison with travel agent community, performs reservation, sales, and advertising functions. Reimbursed by commission on sales, according to individual agreement. The modern cruise industry got its start with Ted Arison, later President and Chairman of Carnival Cruise Lines, acting as General Sales Agent for NCL at its founding.

Germanischer Lloyd
German **classification society**.

GG Group
Guaranteed group – group space allocated to a travel agent.

Give Way

To concede the right-of-way in the interest of avoiding a collision. The "give way" vessel is the ship required to concede the right of way in a crossing or passing situation. The "give way" ship is also referred to as the "burdened" vessel.

Give Way Vessel

See **Give Way**.

Global Maritime Distress and Safety System (GMDSS)

Provides for automatic transmission of a distress signal. This means that a signal will be sent automatically even if, due to an emergency, the crew does not have time to do so.

Global Operator

A cruise line that operates in most major cruising areas throughout the world. Three major global operators are Royal Caribbean International, Holland America Cruises, and Princess Cruises.

Global Positioning System (GPS)

Originally developed by the U.S. government for defence purposes, GPS shows a ship's accurate position anywhere on earth with the help of satellites. The system also illustrates the vessel's position in relation to neighboring islands and other land masses. So comprehensive is the assistance given that officers of the watch need to be reminded to look out the windows occasionally and use that most dependable of all navigational instruments, the naked eye.

Global Voyage

See **World Cruise**.

Globalization

A dominating force in cruising today, the industry has become globalized in three respects: increasing worldwide **cruise ship** deployment; increasing sale of cruises to passengers from many countries regardless of cruise area; and the dominance of cruise markets in a given country by cruise lines based elsewhere, sometimes through a network of wholly- or partially-owned sales networks. A major development is the tendency of operators traditionally based in North America to enhance profits by developing sales networks in Europe, throughout Latin America, and beyond. To a lesser extent, cruise lines traditionally based in Europe have entered the North American market. Two illustrations of globalization: acquisition of a controlling interest in the British tour firm Airtours by Carnival Corporation; and the presence aboard Caribbean **cruise ships** of large groups of Japanese tourists.

GMDSS
See **Global Maritime Distress and Safety System**.

Godmother
The individual chosen to christen or name a ship. Usually a member of royalty, government official, or star of stage and screen, the choice is usually determined by public relations value. The relationship with the ship, however, tends to be a durable one. The naming ceremony now occurs following completion of the vessel. This practice developed when shipyards began to construct ships in **drydock**, a practice that supplanted the high-drama event of a ship's sliding down the **ways** into the water on completion of the **hull**. In the case of the *Grand Princess*, the vessel was christened after its initial series of cruises in the Mediterranean. The event was delayed until the ship reached North America – and the major media markets that would help to determine its success!

GPS
See **Global Positioning Satellite System**.

Grade
Group of cabins with similar, or equivalent characteristics, sold at the same rate. This term is widely used in the UK; in the United States, the equivalent word is **category**.

Grand Dame
A reference to older vessels, frequently former ocean **liners**, that are classics in every sense of the word and still desirable as **cruise ships**. The best example of this is the former Holland America vessel *Rotterdam*, later *Premier's Rembrandt*.

Graving Dock

Drydock built permanently into the shoreline, with concrete walls and gates that open to permit entry and exit of a vessel. This is in contrast with a **floating drydock**, used by many shipyards, that sinks to a certain level when flooded when a ship enters it, and then is pumped dry when the vessel is within so that it floats, like a ship, high in the water. See also **Dry Dock**.

Green Sheet

See **Vessel Sanitation Program (VSP)**.

Green Ship

(1) A ship designed to have no ecological impact from items dumped or discharged at sea; (2) a new ship that is not yet a smooth-running operation from the personnel standpoint because the working relationships of staff have not yet had time to develop. Royal Caribbean's giant Eagle Class ships will be the first "Green Ships" in the environmental sense. While cruise vessels have improved in overboard discharge practices and dumping, none is yet 100% free of these practices at time of writing. Such practices on a modern ship are minimal and regulated by international convention and individual governments. Regarding the use of "green ship" to mean new and untried, modern shipboard management and personnel practices have reduced the "green" period after a ship enters service. The increasing size of cruise fleets gives lines an increasing pool of experienced personnel to draw on when new ships are completed. Also, most new **cruise ships** are twin sisters of at least one previously-built vessel, giving the line previous operational experience with the ship's general configuration. Of course, this does not apply to new companies without either experience or a pool of staff to draw on. In the days of ocean **liners**, it was at least a year following inaugurals before such ships as Italian Line's *Leonardo da Vinci* or Norwegian America Line's *Sagafjord* were completely up to the

standards of their respective companies in cuisine and service. Now, such standards are commonly achieved within several months.

Gross Passenger Per Diem
Income per passenger day before discounts, commissions, and the cost of airfare, transfers, etc.

Gross Register Ton (GRT)
See **Gross Ton**.

Gross Revenue Per Diem
See **Gross Passenger Per Diem**.

Gross Ton
Sometimes referred to as **gross registered ton**, this is a measure of a ship's volume. In general terms, the measure is equal to one hundred cubic feet of space enclosed. This has become the standard way of measuring a ship's size. "Enclosed" is subject to definition and can result in some aberrations of logic in measuring a ship. For instance, a number of factors determine whether a private veranda for a cabin, open to the sea, can be counted. Modern **cruise ships,** which tend to be full-figured rather than long and lean as were the liners of yesteryear, tend to possess large gross tonnage figures. As an example, NCL's *Norway*, formerly the transatlantic liner *France,* remains the longest passenger ship ever built – 1,035 feet long. The length of this 76,049-ton ship substantially exceeds that of the vessel that is currently world's largest – *Grand Princess*, 109,000 gross tons with a length of 951 feet and a **beam** of 118.8 (compared with *Norway's* breadth of 110 feet). These dimensions illustrate the difference between the ocean **liner** breed of passenger ship and the modern cruise vessel. *Norway*, as *France*, was designed to maintain a service speed of thirty-one **knots** in North Atlantic weather, a task that requires different **hull** lines, and greater hull strength, than today's modern **cruise ships** where the prime requirement is a stable platform in reasonably good weather for extensive cabin and public room space.

GSA
See **General Sales Agent**.

Guarantee

Guarantee

Where a passenger is guaranteed a **cabin** in a given category, but is not assigned a specific cabin. This works to the benefit of both cruise line and passenger. For the line, cancellations are very likely to create subsequent availability of accommodation in the category and, in the absence of a guarantee, the booking will likely be lost. If there is no subsequent availability, industry practice is to upgrade the passenger to a higher category at no additional cost. The possibility of this prompts most passengers to accept guarantees. The word among smart consumers is, "Never refuse a guarantee."

Guest

Term adopted by cruise lines for passenger; used both on board ship and in marketing. This marketing-driven term is intended to imply that passengers are treated like guests. It also emphasizes the difference between providing just transportation or a full cruise experience.

Guillotine

Fire door stored in the ceiling that drops in case of fire. RCI's *Voyager of the Seas* will be the first ship to use this technology.

H

Half Ticket

For the purposes of establishing damage awards in case of accident, the first two individuals in a cabin are regarded as **full tickets** whereas third and fourth passengers are regarded as possessing half tickets. These designations do not relate to actual fare paid.

Hang On a Roll

In a cross sea, when a ship reaches the maximum degree of a roll and remains in that same attitude for some seconds, it is said to "hang" on a roll. This tends to happen on ships that are deficient in stability, and can be frightening. This roll characteristic is distinct from ships that have too much stability for comfort, and roll/recover rapidly. Most passenger ships have the degree of stability planned carefully so that motion in a **seaway** is gentle and stately rather than sudden. The best example of a passenger ship hanging on a roll was the first superliner, the 52,117-ton German ship *Imperator*, built in 1912. Even in a calm sea, she would lean a few degrees to one side, only to lean to the other side and then stay there when turning. The situation was resolved when, at the end of the first season in Atlantic service, funnels were shortened, marble bathtubs removed from some accommodation high in the ship, and a great deal of ballast added. A good example of the right degree of stability being built into a ship was French Line's *France*, now the **cruise ship** *Norway*. She remains a very comfortable ship in a rough sea.

Harbor Master

Senior authority in a **port**; assigns berthing location, determines priorities, and controls harbor traffic in general. This can be a complicated logistical enterprise. In the busy port of Piraeus (port for Athens, Greece), the task is not dissimilar to that of air traffic controller. Ships need to register hours, if not days, in advance for time slots. If used on a regular basis, as in every week, reservations for berths are often made years in advance. One of the tools of the trade is the port's **berthing book**, not to be confused with those used in pre-computer days by steamship lines for booking passengers. Policies regarding time slots for an individual **berth** vary greatly from port to port. In many, there is great flexibility regarding when a ship may actually sail. In others, the traffic situation may brook no delay and, regardless of such events as delayed flights, ships must sail at the scheduled hour.

Hard Aground

A ship is sufficiently aground that assistance is required to move the vessel to deep water.

Hardware

This expression usually is used to describe the structure and furnishings of a vessel rather than the **software**, most often used to refer to the cuisine and service. A part of the hardware, ironically, are the **soft furnishings**, or the carpets, bedspreads, cushions, tablecloths, etc.

Hatch

An opening in the deck of a ship, provided for various purposes, with a cover that can be closed. Such openings provide for the loading and unloading of cargo and stores; the servicing and replacement of engine and equipment components, and for emergency escape. Modern ship design has tended to minimize the need for these, a trend accelerated when passenger and **cruise ships** ceased to carry cargo. Now, hatches are to a large extent replaced by side doors. Escape routes are designed into the fundamental access and egress routes within a ship. Hatches were extremely wasteful of space in a passenger ship since, in order to provide access to a deep hold, the hatchway trunk had to penetrate many passenger decks. Aboard the great liners such as *Queen Mary* and *Aquitania*, cargo hatches frequently penetrated some of the highest-density accommodation areas of the ship – this in order to carry a small amount of high-grade cargo. When passenger/cargo ships were converted for cruise or passenger-only operation, areas formerly occupied by hatch trunks became cabin areas and the **holds** to which they provided access, in some cases, became movie theatres and discos.

Hawsepipe

Pipe through which **anchor** chain passes in **bow** or **stern**.

Hawser

A very thick rope, usually of five inches in thickness or more, normally used to secure a ship at **dock** and for other purposes.

Head

(1) Maritime parlance, especially in North America, for a toilet; (2) used as a verb, the direction in which a ship is sailing, *as in to head for*.

Head Sea

The direction of the waves (and, probably, of the wind) is opposite to the course of the ship, creating less comfortable motion conditions than those in a **following sea**. However, the force of wind over the **decks** will be the windspeed plus the ship's speed – something that can make for brisk conditions.

High Density Vessels

Head Tax (Head Fee, or Passenger Tax)

A tax levied by a government, **port authority**, or **port** operator on **cruise ships** for every passenger on board vessels calling at that port. This tax has nothing to do with the number of people actually **disembarking** the vessel. Many ports do not assess head tax; others assess a very high one. In 1997, the highest head tax in the world is assessed in any of the three ports in Bermuda where the tax is $65 per passenger for the usual three-day stay on a seven-day cruise from New York. In contrast, some Caribbean ports charge nothing to encourage **cruise ships** to call, while others assess charges ranging from fifty cents to fifteen dollars. Crew are not included in the count.

Header

Longshoreman in charge of a **gang**.

Heaving Line

See **Messenger Line**.

Helm

Pertaining to the steering of a ship. Refers not to just one element of a ship's steering system, but to the entire system. Thus, if the helm is put hard over, a ship is placed in the position of making a sharp turn. Sometimes, the term by extension is applied to the ship's steering wheel or rudder. One is then left to determine the true meaning by the context.

High Density Vessels

Vessels that have a very high number of passengers per **gross register ton (GRT)**. This is measured in number of gross tons divided by the number of passengers accommodated (basis: two per cabin). See also space ratio. Vessels considered high density vessels are those which have a **space ratio** of about 25 or less. The term was more meaningful in the 1970's when the space ratio was frequently tied to the degree of luxury found on board. The tonnage of ships tended to be less, and cabins, smaller. Also, many **cruise ships,** such as those of NCL and Commodore, had the basic design of an overnight ferry resulting in a high-density ship. Currently, many mass market ships have very attractive space ratios thanks to huge gross tonnage figures resulting from large cabins and extensive public areas. As a consequence, space ratio currently has limited meaning and must be used together with other indicators such as cuisine and service. A ship with a fine food and service reputation but a much lower space ratio may give much greater satisfaction than a vessel with a high number of tons per passenger (the phrase "spacious but lousy", applied to Cunard *Georgic* when she was operated in austerity configuration after World War II, comes to mind). On the other hand, in comparing mass market ships, the ratio may well be a fine indicator of recreational facilities and average cabin size.

High Seas

The ocean beyond the limit of **territorial waters** and the Contiguous Zone established by international treaty. Formerly, the three-mile limit was almost universal, this representing the range of cannon in use during the 1800's. However, there is currently much less standardization.

Hire Purchase

See **Charter Purchase**.

HMS

"His" or "Her Majesty's Ship" – a warship in the British navy. Included here because the name is sometimes applied by the unwary to British merchant ships. The prefix **"RMS"**, on the other hand, connotes a merchant vessel under obligation to the British Crown to carry mail, i.e., a Royal Mail Ship.

Hog

When the center of a ship is on the crest of a wave, the **bow** and **stern** tend to bend lower than the **amidships** section. This ship, under these conditions, is said to hog. See also **Sag**. Some modern **cruise ships,** with their absence of sheer, give the illusion of hogging when in fact they are not. The designers of the latest **cruise ships** have produced hull lines that tend to eliminate this impression.

Hold

Usually applied to a large open area low in the ship that, in ocean **liner** days, would have been used to carry cargo and passenger effects, but in **cruise ships** is used to accommodate supplies and other general storage. Although it can be debated, the luggage **marshaling area** in modern **cruise ships** is perhaps one form of hold and, at times, may be referred to as a hold.

Holding Ground, Good or Bad

Good holding ground is where the bottom of a harbor or anchorage is such that an **anchor** will dig into it and hold the ship in a stationary position. Bad holding ground is just the opposite such that a ship may have to keep engines running in order to help the anchor hold the ship in one place.

Home Base

See **Terminal Port**.

Home port

(1) Traditionally, the **port** in the country of registry to which the shipowners have the closest ties; normally, the name of the port is indicated on the vessel's **stern**; (2) in the cruise era, the port from which a **cruise ship** operates for part of the year, or year-'round. For example, NCL's *Norway* has been based in Miami for years; on the other hand, Royal Caribbean's *Nordic Empress* is home-ported in San Juan for part of the year and in Port Canaveral for the balance; (3) in this **flag of convenience** era, the **port of registry** – most often, the major port in the country of registry. In modern colloquial usage, the term home base or terminal port is also frequently used.

Horsepower

The power needed to lift 33,000 pounds one foot in one minute; alternatively, that needed to lift one pound 550 feet in one second. The abbreviation for horsepower is HP. In the cruise industry, this generic term is commonly used to denote the power of main engines as well as of **bow** and **stern thrusters**.

Hospitality Purser

Individual in the purser's department of some

cruise lines responsible for dealing directly with passengers, or of supervising staff who do.

Host Program

Programs offered by some cruise lines for enhancing the cruise satisfaction of unescorted women on board. Hosts must be good dancers, have good manners, and be well-dressed. They are expected to divide their time among the various ladies on board. Typically, they have a bar allowance and some reimbursement for other expenses. They are forbidden from entering into romantic relationships with those on board, though this is difficult to enforce. Basically, working as a host is a means for these gentlemen to work their way on cruises. One of the first companies to offer this amenity on an organized scale was Royal Cruise Line (subsequently purchased by NCL and later, dropped as a separate **brand**).

Hot Work

Refers to work involving welding. This is a high-risk activity and, among other accidents, led to the loss of French Line's *Normandie* by fire in 1942. At the time, the vessel was being converted into the American troop ship *Lafayette*. Not only were fire-suppressing systems not in operation, but also, there was a general state of disorganization on board. Most cruise lines are required to take special care when hot work is undertaken. There is frequently special fire equipment on standby and an observing officer on hand. Preferably, hot work is left for overhaul periods. So vital is this area for safety that procedures are specified by the **classification society** *and* the owner of the **drydock** where work is often undertaken.

Hotel Manager

This is a typical designation for the senior hotel official on board a **cruise ship**. His duties may include comprehensive responsibility for all food, service, and entertainment on board. Tables of organization, however, differ from line to line and there is no hard-and-fast rule regarding responsibilities attached to this position. Invariably, responsibilities are extensive. Although the term is associated with the modern **cruise ship** era, it was adopted by the Cunard Line in the late 1960's.

Hotel Officers

Personnel who supervise the hotel functions of a ship. The titles and responsibilities of the positions comprising the hotel officers vary from cruise line to cruise line and from nationality to nationality. Commonly used titles include but are not limited to: **hotel manager, chief steward, food and bar manager, maitre'd, head waiter**, and **chief purser**.

Hull

The water-tight portion of a ship's skin, the part that causes the ship to float in the water. The plates that form the hull are collectively known as **shell plating**. One of the main strength elements of a vessel's structure, the hull encloses much of the accommodation and machinery and supports the **superstructure**. The design of a hull is critical to a ship's speed, general performance, and stability. At times, several quite different classes of **cruise ship** will share variations of a similar hull design. An example: Holland America's *Statendam* Class and Costa's *CostaClassica* and *CostaRomantica*, both classes built by Fincantieri.

Hull Down

Due to the curvature of the earth, only the **mast, funnel**, and **superstructure** of a distant ship are visible. The **hull** is obscured by the earth's curve.

Hull Insurance

Also referred to as **Hull** and **Machinery** Insurance. Covers not only the main engines, but usually also all equipment on board such as that in kitchens, laundries, elevators, and on the bridge.

Hull & Machinery

A term used in insurance that, normal meanings aside, is used to refer to coverage for the ship itself, including furnishings, equipment, and the structure of the ship. Historically, hull & machinery coverage also included partial liability coverage, referred to as "the running down clause."

Hull Number

As soon as construction starts on a new ship, a hull number is assigned. It becomes a part of the vessel's permanent record on the certificate of registry and is frequently used to refer to the vessel during construction by shipyard personnel. Once the ship has a name, this is used instead of the hull number.

I

I.T.V.
See **Interactive Television**.

ICCL
See **International Council of Cruise Lines (ICCL)**.

Immersion Suit
A nearly-watertight suit covering the entire body except the face, it is worn to prevent heat-loss in cold water or under conditions of exposure to cold wind, spray, or precipitation. Provided in lifeboats for crew who, in modern lifeboats, occupy a more exposed position than other occupants (most cruise ship lifeboats are partially enclosed). **SOLAS** regulations specify number of immersion suits to be provided in lifeboats; the circumstances under which they are to be available; and the performance specifications that immersion suits must meet. Ships operating year-round in warm water are exempt from this requirement with permission of **IMO** administration.

IMO
See **International Maritime Organization**.

IMO Number
See **Ship Identification Number**.

In Bond
Cargo or supplies within the custody of customs or customs-approved bailee – often referred to as a bonded warehouse.

In Class
A ship's status, based on design and condition, where a ship conforms to the requirements for a given class of vessel as determined by a **Classification Society**. This is a major issue for insurance underwriters who will probably not insure an unclassified vessel. When a ship is extensively

refitted, those planning the refit must ensure that the ship remains in class following the refurbishing or rebuilding. When a vessel is laid up or used, for instance, as a stationary accommodation ship, a **captain** must be on board and such items as pressure on the fire extinguishing system must be maintained if the ship is to remain in class. If a **cruise ship** falls out of class, when it is returned to "in class" status it must meet all current requirements with grandfather clauses, if any, null and void.

In Soundings

A ship is in soundings when close enough to shore to ascertain the water depth through normal soundings using an echo sounder. The hundred-fathom line (when the sea depth decreases to a hundred **fathoms** or less) is the traditional point at which a vessel, inbound, is within soundings.

In-Cabin Calling

The ability to make long distance telephone calls from one's **cabin**. Until the early nineties, most vessels did not have this capability. Those wanting to use a telephone had to go to the radio room. Satellite technology now allows for easy installation of satellite dishes on board ship making in-cabin calling an easy amenity to provide.

In-Cabin Magazine

A special publication for the ship or cruise line that promotes shipboard activities; products sold on board ship; ports of call; and sometimes more general information not directly related to the forgoing. It may also contain travel tips, local recipes, and profiles of local personalities. Contents vary from line to line. Format is usually high-gloss and high-color.

Inaugural Book

Inaugural books are produced when a new ship enters service. Generally a hard-back publication, it describes the design and construction of the ship; and profiles designers, builders, cruise line executives, and usually the cruise line itself. It is financed by advertisements of cruise line suppliers and venders associated with the construction of the ship, and also ports of call.

Inaugural Cruise
See **Maiden Voyage**.

Inboard
Toward the center of a ship; away from the side. Indicates a direction or relative location.

INCHARPASS
A passenger charter agreement developed in 1967 by the Institute of Chartered Ship brokers used as the basis for passenger ship charters.

Inclined
SOLAS mandates that all **passenger ships** of more than twenty-four meters in length must be inclined on completion to determine stability characteristics. The **Master** is then given the information that he requires to calibrate stability under normal service conditions by adjusting **ballast**.

Incombustible Material
See **Noncombustible Material**.

Indemnity Bond
An agreement whereby a cruise line is held to be free of liability.

Infirmary
Ship's medical facility.

Informal Dress
When used as a recommended style of dress for an evening aboard ship, usually means a jacket or suit and tie for men and pantsuit or dress for women.

INMARSAT
See **International Maritime Satellite System**.

Inside Cabin
See **Cabin**.

Inside Passage
Natural waterway between Vancouver, B.C. and Juneau, Alaska that is highly scenic and a feature of almost all cruises to Alaska. The passage is protected from the open ocean by a series of offshore islands.

Inside Sales
An office in cruise line headquarters that assists sales representatives in the field. Typical functions include assistance with correspondence, help with special requests, the organization of **cruise nights**,

requests for special rates, **fam trips**, and service to small agencies without a designated **district sales manager**.

Integrated Bridge

(1) An integrated electronic navigation system combining radar, autopilot, and positioning devices; (2) when the structure of a ship's **bridge** is integrated into the main body of the **superstructure**. In the first decades of this century, the bridge was often in a separate structure of its own forward of the main superstructure mass in a mode of design called an island bridge. This was adopted to give officers separation from passengers and to provide space for a cargo hatch between the bridge and main superstructure. The space in between the two sections of the superstructure was known as the "virgin's leap." This was in the days when line passenger ships carried large amounts of cargo. Most of the ships constructed for Cunard, White Star, Royal Mail, and many other companies before and immediately after World War I had this arrangement. The practice died as superstructures became more streamlined and the bridge became an integrated part of it. The term is especially applicable to modern **cruise ships** where the bridge is completely enclosed and air-conditioned (no **bridge wings** open to the air) and therefore an integral part of the superstructure.

Interactive Television (I.T.V.)

Allows passengers using the in-cabin TV to order movies, purchase shore excursions, write e-mail, view dinner menus, shipboard account status, and undertake many more functions without leaving the cabin. This has become quite common since the mid-1990's. Applications will become increasingly universal as the technology and a line's ability to provide the interface advance.

Intergovernmental Maritime Consultative Organization

See **International Maritime Organization (IMO)**.

Interim Rule

The Coast Guard, from time to time, issues rules relating to a number of areas within its jurisdictional authority that are distributed to all cruise lines. These interim rules may be distributed among **IMO's** Maritime Safety Committee for debate/comment and potential international action.

International Code of Signals

Code of approved signals at sea, currently administered by **IMO**. Includes the shape and color of flags and their meaning. The first such code was initiated in 1817.

International Council of Cruise Lines (ICCL)

The Washington, D.C.-based association, under the direction of industry chief executives of member lines, advocates industry positions to key domestic and international regulatory organizations, policymakers, and industry partners, and participates in the regulatory and policy development process. Its predecessor organization, the ICPL, was founded in 1967 in New York. In 1997, ICCL established an Associate Member program, opening council membership to the cruise industry's strategic business partners. The ICCL actively monitors international shipping policy and develops recommendations for its membership on a wide variety of issues. The Council is comprised of the nineteen largest cruise lines that call at major ports in the U.S. and abroad.

International Labor Organization (ILO) Maritime Conference

The ILO convened a maritime conference in 1997 focused on laying down basic guidelines regarding working conditions aboard ship. Eight hundred delegates from eighty-five countries agreed to adopt three sets of conventions and related recommendations, together with one protocol, all by a large majority. These standards rely on local governmental authorities for enforcement. The conventions, recommendations, and protocol include the following: Work hours not to exceed fourteen hours in any twenty-four hour period, or seventy-two hours in a seven-day period; periods of rest must be at least ten hours long in a twenty-four hour period and seventy-seven hours in a seven-day period; hours of rest may be divided into only two periods, one of which must be at least six hours long; the interval between consecutive periods of rest cannot be more than fourteen hours. The minimum age for working aboard a ship was raised from fourteen to sixteen. These rules are to be posted in an easily-accessible place aboard ship, and records of work schedules are to be maintained.

International Lifesaving Appliance Code (LSA)
Contains requirements for lifesaving gear in ships with a **construction date** (with actual assembly of metal beginning) after July 1 1998. These may be found in **SOLAS**, 1995 and 1996 amendments.

International Load Line Certificate
Certificate issued by **classification society** or flag **administration** confirming the information on the vessel's **Plimsoll** marking i.e. how deeply laden the ship may be under a variety of sea conditions and/or geographical areas such as: in salt water, fresh water, winter North Atlantic, etc.

International Maritime Organization (IMO)
The IMO is a consultative and advisory board of the United Nations which was established in 1948 to review current maritime issues and set international commercial shipping policy. The IMO's stated purpose is to provide a forum for cooperation among governments in the field of governmental regulation and practices relating to technical matters affecting shipping engaged in international trade, to encourage the adoption of the highest practicable standards in matters concerning maritime safety and the prevention and control of marine pollution from ships, to encourage the removal of discriminatory action and unnecessary restrictions by governments affecting shipping engaged in international trade, and to consider unfair restrictive shipping practices. The IMO has a special responsibility and interest in the safety of life at sea, protecting the environment through prevention of pollution and environmental damage caused by vessels. The IMO has been instrumental in the adoption of a variety of important conventions, including **SOLAS** and the International Convention for the Prevention of Pollution from Ships.

International Maritime Satellite System

The **IMO** at its assembly meeting in 1973 decided to establish an International Maritime Satellite System to allow communication among vessels. In July of 1979, INMARSAT was officially formed and has over 40 participating member countries. The services provided by INMARSAT include a telex, telephone, fax, transfer of data, telegram, distress calls, weather and navigation information, and other data. In recent years, many cruise lines have developed their own satellite communication systems and are relying less on the international system which, however, still exists. For companies with their own systems, INMARSAT serves as an important backup.

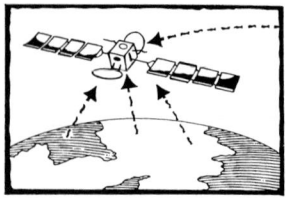

International Nautical Mile

See **Nautical Mile**.

International Safety Management Code (ISM Code)

The Code arose from concern with poor standards of management in the shipping industry. In 1989, **IMO** adopted guidelines for shipboard management aimed at achieving high safety standards and competent efforts to prevent pollution. Adherence became mandatory through a 1994 amendment in **SOLAS**. See also **Safety Management System (SMS)**.

International Tonnage Certificate

Certificate issued by flag administration or **classification society** confirming a ship's tonnage figures.

International Transport Workers Federation (ITF)

Free trade union body, sponsored by many individual maritime unions, that represents the interest of transport workers and worker unions throughout the world. Counsels workers on flag-of-convenience ships. Brings pressure to bear on cruise lines to improve working conditions.

Introduction Costs

The costs associated with introducing a new vessel to the market. These include all operating expenses for the ship during the time that complimentary cruises are offered, special events, special advertising, etc. Generally, this is part of the sales and marketing budget.

Inventory Control
Operations-level function that implements the directives of those working in **yield management**. Inventory Control is usually a function of Reservations Administration.

ISM Code
See **International Safety Management Code**.

Issuing Carrier
Applied to the cruise industry, the line issuing travel documents in the form of a passage ticket or publishing a list of rates.

ITF
See **International Transport Workers Federation**.

Itinerary
Ports of call on a given cruise, including their order, and the schedule for arrivals and departures in each.

J

Jacob's Ladder
A rope ladder with wooden steps that is attached to the side of the vessel allowing **crew** members to get on and off a ship. Frequently used to transfer to a small boat, and by **pilots** when an accommodation ladder is not available.

Jetsam
See **Flotsam and Jetsam**.

Jettison
To throw an item overboard. This term most frequently describes this action taken to lighten the ship when it is in danger, but it can be used in other circumstances e.g. to dispose of spoiled items.

Jetty
In Europe, common name for a pier or quay.

JIT
"Just in time." A form of inventory control that does not replenish supplies until those on hand are virtu-

ally exhausted. This is the least expensive form of inventory control inasmuch as it reduces the cost of warehousing, reduces investment in inventory, etc. The risks are obvious. However, the cost savings can be considerable. In the cruise industry, this helps eliminate the need for food store rooms ashore.

Jones Act

Enacted in 1920, section 33 of the Merchant Marine Act is commonly referred to as the "Jones Act." It provides remedies to seamen injured due to the negligence of the vessel owner, **master,** or fellow **crew** members. It also contains provisions governing United States coastwise trade. The "Jones Act" label is widely misused to the extent that it has entered the language as embracing provisions that do not, in reality, exist in this act. For example, it is frequently confused with the Passenger Services Act (PSA) which regulates passenger traffic in the cruise industry (U.S. Code, Section 282, Transportation of Passengers in Foreign Vessels). Actually the Merchant Marine Act of 1920, provides for the promotion and maintenance of the American Merchant Marine. It requires that transportation of merchandise between U.S. ports be done by ships that were built (or in some circumstances refurbished) in the United States, that are 75% U.S.-owned, operated with U.S. crew and officers, and fly the U.S. flag. Though referred to frequently as the act that regulates passenger traffic in the cruise industry, it is Title 46 of the U.S. Code, Section 282, Transportation of Passengers in Foreign Vessels, that actually regulates the cruise industry. See also **Passenger Services Act (PSA)**.

Joystick

A lever that enables the officer of the watch to control the direction and speed of a ship, used when entering and leaving **port**. This allows for simultaneous control of propulsion machinery, **rudders, propellers**, and **thrusters** in a completely coordinated manner, obviating the need to issue separate orders for each or to manipulate separate controls. Joysticks are often present not only in the central **bridge** area but on each of the **bridge wings** as well, useful when maneuvering.

Jumboising
See **Stretching**.

Jury-Rig
An improvisation used when there is damage to a ship or equipment failure. A jury **mast**, for instance, is one erected in place of a permanent one that has carried away. The "jury rigged" substitute is used until a ship reaches **port** or until permanent repairs can be made.

K

Keel
The backbone of a ship, the longest continuous girder or line of plates at the bottom of the vessel. This is the strongest part of a ship. Before all-welded and prefabricated construction, the keel was the focal point of ribs extending to the top of the **hull** and to which the vessel's steel plates were rivetted. Now, ships are assembled in pieces much like a child's Lego blocks. The main keel is most often supplemented by additional keels. A **bilge** keel, at the turn of the bilge, or where the hull begins to curve upward, serves as a fin to reduce **rolling**. When reference is made to a keel being laid, this means that the actual construction of the **cruise ship** has begun.

Keel Draft
See **Extreme Draft**.

Key (Cay)
Generic name for a small island in the area of the West Indies.

Kingpost
Cargo handling mast system consisting of two vertical posts abreast connected with a horizontal steel member above. On passenger ships that also carried cargo, this provided a compact arrangement of booms and **masts** that was rigid and minimized

topside clutter. It was a design feature of many ocean **liners** of the Thirties through the Fifties that also carried a quantity of cargo.

Knot

(1) The primary unit of speed in navigation, equal to one nautical mile per hour. A speed of one knot is equal to 1.15 land miles per hour; (2) one of various ways of tying a rope to itself or around a fixture.

L

L-Shaped Cabin (Bibby Cabin)

A **cabin** mainly located **inboard** but with a section that reaches to the side of the ship making it possible for the room to have a **porthole** or window. In ocean **liner** days, also referred to as a Bibby cabin after the steamship line that invented them. The company was able to claim that all cabins were outside in that they had **portholes**. The feature was soon copied by most other steamship lines offering tropical services. The Bibby Line provided sailings every two weeks from Great Britain to Burma in the days of the British Empire. Most modern cruise companies, encouraged by current construction methods, opt for either completely inside or completely outside rooms. The Bibby concept was efficient when cabins were built in the shipyard individually on board a ship. Now, they are generally built in factories and are of standard shape and size to minimize cost.

Labor Inspection (Seafarers) Convention, 1996 (No. 178)

See **International Labor Organization Maritime Conference.**

Laid Up

A ship that is not in operation. The vessel may be outdated, awaiting a new assignment, or awaiting refurbishing. Some ships are laid up seasonally, as with many Greek operators in the Mediterranean during the winter. However, the only really profitable option is to operate a **cruise ship** on a year-round basis. Aside from covering fixed costs, it is important to retain skilled staff and not have to undertake annual training and orientation at the completion of layup. It is essential to keep a ship **in class** during layup by having a **captain** on board, maintaining pressure in the fire control system, and by meeting other requirements of keeping a ship in its existing class. Failure to do this can mean that on re-entry into passenger service, all current requirements of class must be met; any grandfather provisions are null and void.

Late Sitting
See **Sittings, Late and Early.**

Launch
In the old days, the process of moving a ship from its place of initial construction on land to water by having it slide down the **ways**, a series of rails connecting the building area with the water. This was a dramatic but high-risk operation. Currently, ships are built in **drydock** and floated out for final completion. A derivative of this term, relaunched, wrongly used by some writers and PR officials, refers to a ship's reentry into service following a refurbishing or renaming. In fact, a ship is launched only once, if at all.

Layup
See **Laid Up.**

Lead Agent
Senior agent in a reservations, inside sales, or group department who supervises the work of those within the functional area.

Lead Service
Also referred to as lead referral, this service provides follow-up for major sales prospects, such as potential incentive or other groups. The Service has a sales team that scans cruise industry business sources and provides information to a cruise line for a fee.

Leg
Segment of a cruise between two ports. It is most frequently used to describe the **"final leg"** prior to return to the port in which the ship is based.

Lengthening
See **Stretching.**

Dictionary of the Cruise Industry

Length Overall (LOA)

Total length, including any incidental structure that may extend this dimension. "Overall" is sometimes used to describe other dimensions as well.

Letter of Intent

Outlines the basic features of a planned transaction. Often mentioned in connection with building a new ship, but sometimes also in connection with the purchase of a ship or company. It is not a binding contract, but does outline the most important elements of the proposed transaction including cost, basic characteristics of the proposed vessel, and when it will be completed. This then clears the way for obtaining financing, performing due diligence, and other matters relating to what will eventually be a firm contract. The term **memorandum of understanding** is also sometimes used.

LHWCA

See **Long Shore and Harbor Workers Compensation Act.**

Lido Deck

Usually used to refer to an area rather than to a complete **deck**, it is a space containing a swimming pool, deck chairs, bar, and everything else needed to relax in the sun. A lido area may be **amidships** and open to the sky (enclosed on all four sides); or in its traditional location high in the **stern**, sheltered from the wind forward but open to the ocean aft. A number of **cruise ships** do have complete decks named for this feature, usually containing a lido area but, frequently, other features as well such as cabins and public rooms.

Lien

See **Maritime Lien.**

Life Preservers

Personal flotation device (PFD) worn by an individual passenger or member of ship's staff in emergency situations. Number, availability, manner of use, and orientation of passengers and crew regarding correct use are covered in **SOLAS** regulations.

Lifeboat/Liferaft Launching

Life Raft

An inflatable or rigid flotation device or raft which supplements the lifesaving capacity of a ship's life boats. Most of those used on passenger ships are of the inflatable type and can inflate automatically when launched from a ship.

Life Ring

Personal flotation device, usually in the shape of a ring, required to be readily accessible on open decks and on both sides of a vessel. They can't be permanently secured, and must be ready to be cast loose e.g. to a person who has fallen overboard. **SOLAS** regulations specify requirements for availability of lifebuoys with the following accessories: buoyant lifelines, self-igniting lights, self-igniting smoke signals, and their placement. See SOLAS regulations for further details.

Lifeboat Drill

All passengers must participate in this drill on departure aboard a **short international voyage (SOLAS)** or within twenty-four hours of departure on a longer trip. Passengers and selected **crew** must go to muster stations on the sounding of the **general emergency alarm** where they are instructed on appropriate emergency clothing and given instructions concerning emergency procedures and responsibilities. For all applicable procedures, see **SOLAS** regulations.

Lifeboat Launching, Float-Free

A mode of lifeboat launching where the boat floats free, ready to use, after the deck on which it rests sinks below water level.

Lifeboat Launching, Free-Fall

Where a lifeboat (really an enclosed life raft) with occupants is allowed to fall to the water's surface from a ship. There are no restraining ropes, etc.

Lifeboat/Liferaft Launching

Launching methods for lifeboats and liferafts include the following: with conventional davits, one of the most visible features of a modern **cruise ship**; free-fall using enclosed rafts and ramp; float-free, where the boat or raft floats free after the deck is immersed. Provision for launching lifeboats must be made even with a maximum **trim** of ten degrees and a **list**, either way, of twenty degrees. **SOLAS** regulations are the authority for the many rules that apply.

Lifejacket (Life Preserver)

Buoyant vest that keeps its occupant afloat, upright, with mouth clear of water even if unconscious. Must have limited fire resistance. Requirements are many and detailed and are found in **SOLAS** regulations. **Cruise ships** are required to have more than enough for all passengers and **crew**, with a number equal to 5% of those on board to be stowed on open decks or at muster stations in newly-constructed vessels.

Lifesaving Equipment

See **Personal Lifesaving Appliances**.

Light Draft

See **Draft**.

Light Ice Class Hull

Ships with light ice class designation can sail in waters with sufficient floating ice that the ice segments, though broken, touch each other. In contrast, an icebreaker sails in areas where the ice is solid. Examples of ships with light ice class designations are the *Marco Polo*, of Orient Lines and the *Explorer* of Abercrombie & Kent.

Lightweight

Actual weight of the ship itself, i.e. without cargo, fuel, lubricating oil, ballast, fresh water, consumable stores, passengers, crew, and baggage.

Lightweight Tonnage

Actual weight of a ship – one that is completely empty i.e. free of stores, fuel, cargo, etc.

Line

A rope that is fastened and functional, i.e. "…a rope with a job."

Line Man

An employee of the port, or of a **port contractor**, who handles mooring ropes on shore when a ship docks or sails. On arrival, a thin **heaving line** attached to a major mooring rope is thrown ashore. The heavier rope attached to it is then pulled ashore and attached to a **bollard** in order to secure a vessel to the pier.

Line Voyage

A voyage in which the object is to provide transportation from one point to another. In industry usage, this is the opposite of the term **"cruise."**

Liner

In the old days, a vessel designed to provide one-way point-to-point transportation for passengers and, generally, limited cargo. Liners usually had more than one class for passengers with separate dining rooms, lounges, and deck areas for each. Both speed and general characteristics, including class configuration, were designed to meet the requirements of a given route. Currently, the term is also used to denote a cargo ship that sails on a regular schedule. See also **Classic Cruise Ship**.

List

When a vessel, due to improper **ballast** or damage, leans toward **port** or **starboard**.

LLL

See **Low Level Lighting**.

Lloyd's List

An international daily shipping newspaper established in 1734, Lloyd's List is one of the oldest daily newspapers in the world. The publication started in an era when maritime signaling was limited to visual signals and reporting the safe arrival of ships was an important function. Its pages now are unique in containing virtually comprehensive reports on marine casualties, as well as an enormous amount of other information on shipping.

Lloyd's Register of Shipping

A leading **classification society** founded in 1760. Currently includes approximately 21% of the world's tonnage. Annually produces a three-volume Register of Ships giving all ship particulars. The organization is commonly abbreviated LR.

LOA
See **Length Overall (LOA)**.

Load Draft
See **Draft**.

Load Factor
Average percentage of a ship's accommodation that is occupied, based on the number of lower beds. Load factors are often in excess of 100% aboard ships with a substantial number of upper berths that tend to be occupied.

Log
Best known log is the general and navigational record, required of all ships in service, recording on a **watch**-to-watch basis all phenomenon and events related to a vessel's navigation and significant events on board. It functions as a manual equivalent to an airplane's "black box." It records such things as course, speed, information on weather conditions as well as **deck and engine** developments of note. **SOLAS** also mandates notations, together with time, of the closing of all openings in the side of the ship prior to sailing. In addition to the general log referenced here, a number of other logs must be maintained. These include those required by covering such areas as garbage handling, oil and sludge removal, and other items. In addition, individual cruise lines require the keeping of other logs for a variety of purposes.

Logo Shop
Profitable source of on board revenue aboard a **cruise ship**. Merchandise is made up of items with the name of the ship and/or company. Logo merchandise may also be sold by mail order catalog.

Longitudinal Cross Section
Cross section of a ship laid out in a **fore**-and-**aft** direction. This can be of an area or of an entire ship.

Longshore and Harbor Workers Compensation Act (LHWCA)
This Act provides workers' compensation benefits to maritime workers other than seamen working

Low Speed Diesel

Engine used in many **cruise ships** currently in service where speeds range from 100 to 250 RPM.

Low-Location Lighting (LLL)

Strips of lights low in a corridor or other area that defines emergency escape routines from a ship's interior for passengers. Since smoke tends to rise and obscure other indicators, these lights, similar to those in aircraft, function under conditions of visibility obscured by smoke. **SOLAS** (Resolution A.752(18) defines and prescribes the nature, placement, testing, and maintenance of these.

Lower Berth

In current usage, not a **berth** at all but a single bed of standard height. The number of lower berths determines the vessel's normal capacity. Frequently, these may be placed together to form a double or queen-sized bed. In the days of ocean **liners** and **line voyages**, a distinction could be made between a standard berth and standard bed: the berth was narrower and fixed to the floor and wall. For generations, to travel on an ocean steamship was to sleep in a berth rather than a bed. Beds were reserved for deluxe accommodation.

LR

See **Lloyd's Register of Shipping**.

LSA

See **International Lifesaving Appliance Code**.

Lying Off

Vessel waiting for pier space and either anchored offshore or drifting, with position being roughly held by manipulation of engines.

M

Machinery Plant

Lay term for main engines and major associated machinery. Often used to include all machinery including air conditioning system, electrical generators, etc. This is not a very exact term; it is prefer-

Machinery Spaces

able to use more descriptive phrases such as main engines, refrigeration plant, etc.

Machinery Spaces

As used in **SOLAS**, includes spaces that hold main propulsion machinery, machinery used for other purposes with a power output of at least 375 KW, and spaces containing any oil-fired boiler or oil fuel unit; that house steam and combustion engines, generators, oil-filling stations, machinery for refrigerating, stabilizing, ventilation and airconditioning equipment, other similar spaces, and trunks to these spaces.

Maiden Voyage

First voyage with commercial passengers. Generally does not include preinaugural familiarization trips for travel agents and travel press. In any case, preinaugurals generally take the form of one- or two-night cruises to nowhere although segments of the delivery voyage from shipyard to **home port** may be used for this purpose. The maiden voyage is also sometimes referred to as the inaugural cruise.

Main Generating Station

As used in **SOLAS**, the location of the **main source of electrical power**.

Main Source of Electrical Power

SOLAS term for the machinery that supplies electrical power to the main switchboard for distribution throughout the ship such that the vessel will be in **normal operational and habitable condition**.

Main Vertical Zones

Defined by major fire and/or watertight **bulkheads**, "**A Class Divisions**," that have doors to maintain passenger access. **SOLAS** regulations specify that the distance between bulkheads may not exceed forty meters or one hundred twenty feet. Main vertical zones are tied to passenger and **crew** escape routes which also must be approved. In addition, vessels sailing from U.S. **ports** must meet Coast Guard standards which differ in detail from those issued by **IMO**.

Make Whole Costs

Those incurred by a cruise line when, thanks to a

cancelled sailing, the line is unable to provide a cruise that has been paid for.

Managing Owner

When there are several owners of a company, the owner to whom the management of the firm has been entrusted.

Manhole

An opening in an engine, crankcase, double bottom, etc. large enough to allow a person to pass through it. These are provided to facilitate maintenance.

Manifest

List of passengers and/or crew on board at a given time. Normally, labeled "Passenger Manifest" and "Crew Manifest" or "Passenger and Crew Manifest." Manifests are needed for dealing with customs, immigration, internal accounting including passenger expenditures aboard the vessel, and to meet other requirements of local governments. Requirements vary greatly from **port** to port and country to country. For instance, in China manifests are required in Chinese and English Languages. Most ports require languages using the western alphabet. In some cases, electronic versions are accepted and can be transmitted in advance.

Manifest, Ship's

Document almost universally required by customs and immigration authorities listing passenger and crew names, nationalities, and passport numbers. Currently, it is often transmitted electronically to port authorities in advance of arrival.

Manning Guide

See **Manning Scale**.

Manning Scale

Crew required to operate the ship safely. Traditionally referring primarily to deck and engine areas, also currently used for hotel departments to specify staff required for routine operation under given circumstances.

Mare Clausum

Territorial waters falling within the jurisdiction of a country and subject to the laws of that nation. The opposite of "high seas" or **mare liberum**. The territorial waters issue is a major one for the cruise industry in that restrictions on such activities as gambling are often imposed on ships operating within them.

Mare Liberum
High seas, subject to international maritime law. See also **High Seas**.

Margin Line
When a ship is in damaged condition, the highest permissible location on the side of a vessel that the water may reach in the final condition of sinkage, trim and heel following defined damage i.e. single or double-compartment flooding. This calculated point is critical in relation to the vessel's status as a one- or two-compartment ship. The water level in no case is permitted to be less than three inches (76 mm) below the top of the **bulkhead** deck at the side. In some vessels, the subdivision of one portion of the ship may be calculated to one margin line while that of the balance of the ship may be calculated to another.

Marine Hotel Association (MHA)
International trade organization consisting of over two hundred cruise lines and suppliers of the products and services they use. Founded in 1985, MHA is a not-for-profit organization serving as a forum for discussion regarding issues of concern to the community of suppliers and the lines they serve. Activities include an annual conference and trade show, a scholarship program for cruise line personnel, and a quarterly newsletter.

Marine League
Three nautical miles.

Marine Operation
Used to denote that side of a cruise line's operation relating to the navigation of the fleet. Embraces such areas as crewing, maintenance, safety, fueling, and appointment/ evaluation of officers. Refers to a category of company operations and is a general term.

Marine Polution Control Unit (MPCU)
Unit within the British Coastguard Agency responsible for activities and countermeasures relating to pollution.

Maritime Security Council (MSC)

Marine Safety Agency (MSA)
Unit within the British Department of Transport responsible for maritime safety.

Marine Salvage
A broad term involving a network of activities related to recovery of a vessel that has been sunk or damaged. This may involve the raising of a ship, towing, recovery of cargo. Most countries control these activities in territorial waters, in some cases actually contracting for salvage.

Maritime Law
A highly general term applied to international and national statutes, treaties, and judge-made law pertaining to the operation of ships, **harbors, crew**, and passengers. Much of what is known as maritime law has its foundations in British **Admiralty Law** which is not a fixed legal corpus but a series of judicial decisions made over the years. Of course, individual nations have added their own legal adjuncts and variations as well as, inevitably, conflicts and inconsistencies.

Maritime Lien
The placing of a **lien** on a ship, enforceable by arrest, which paves the way for selling a vessel to pay debts incurred if these are not otherwise discharged. It commences a process whereby a ship may be sold to other owners free and clear and the proceeds distributed among creditors. The bankruptcy of Regency Cruises was triggered when a caterer placed a lien on the *Regent Rainbow* in Tampa because of a major balance owed to them. In recent years, several Commonwealth of Independent States vessels were arrested because of unpaid bills. Those chartering passenger ships should make themselves aware of the financial status of owners to avoid unexpected arrest of a ship and major financial loss by the charterer. However, liens are threatened and may be placed to prompt payment of even minor debts, e.g. payment of back wages for an individual member of a ship's staff. Although not usually used in this manner, a ship mortage is a voluntary lien.

Maritime Security Council (MSC)
Council of cruise lines, port authorities, **P & I clubs**,

maritime vendors, and others to improve marine security. The group deals with terrorism, drug trafficking, stowaways, and other security-related matters.

Maritime Telephone Area Codes

There are four public-use satellites handling maritime calls, each with its own area code. Codes are as follows: for the Eastern Atlantic, 871; the Western Atlantic, 874; the Pacific, 872; the Indian Ocean, 873.

MARPOL

The international convention for the prevention of pollution from ships. It was published in 1973, modified in 1978. It is better known as MARPOL 73-78. This is the most important international agreement on the subject of marine pollution. It handles not only pollution from oil, but also pollution from chemicals and other harmful substances such as garbage and sewage. MARPOL does not cover all **IMO** conventions regarding oil pollution. For example, OPARC (Oil Pollution Preparedness Response and Cooperation) is a separate convention.

MARPOL Certificate

Certificate issued by the flag country or classification society that confirms vessel compliance with **MARPOL** requirements.

Marquee Value

Inclusion of a port in an itinerary because its appeal is sufficiently great as to enhance the attractiveness of the entire cruise. **Ports** with high "marquee value" include St. Thomas for cruises to the Eastern Caribbean; St. Petersburg for sailings to the Baltic; and Glacier Bay, for Alaska cruises.

Marshaling Area

Open work area generally low in a ship's **hull** used to bring on board, or prepare to place ashore, luggage, supplies, equipment, etc.

Mass Market (Contemporary Cruise Market Segment)

Modern cruising's largest market segment, it includes most of the capacity in the cruise industry. Major players include Carnival, Princess (short cruises), and Royal Caribbean. Mass market lines dominate cruises to popular destinations such as the Caribbean, Mexican Riviera, and Alaska. Food and service is of standard rather than of deluxe quality, though accommodation and entertainment is frequently among the best in the industry. Minimum fares are usually just over $100 per day per person, double. Momentum in this market segment is responsible for most industry growth and profitability. Common designation of this product category in-house at cruise lines is "contemporary cruise market segment."

Mast

Vertical pole on a ship used to carry sails in the days of sailing ships and currently used to mount radar and radio equipment. The four raked masts carried by some early passenger liners have given way to one stream-lined post over the **bridge** to carry modern navigational and radio equipment.

Master

Official term for **Captain**. Even when a subordinate officer temporarily takes the place of a captain e.g. in the event of the master's illness, the individual designated is the captain or master rather than the post normally held. There must always be a Master on board to maintain a ship in **Class**.

Master-at-Arms

Security Officer.

Material Risk

Essential risk-related factors that an insurance company has the right to know before insuring a vessel.

Maximum Medical Care

The greatest amount a cruise line can pay a crew member for medical expenses, by policy.

Maximum Speed

Generally, the speed a ship is capable of making with all boilers on line or all diesels in operation at maximum power. Ships normally do not sustain this speed for an entire voyage. Engines have to be taken off line for routine maintenance, as do boilers. Therefore, a ship's maximum cruising speed is a truer index of how fast the ship really is. On the other hand, in emergency situations, most ships can reach impressive speed for short periods. This is especially true of turbine steamships that can be "forced" – operated at steam pressures above the usual maximum in the face of an urgent requirement.

Mayday
See **Distress Signal**.

Mean Time Between Failures
Standard phrase to measure the dependability of equipment.

MedCruise
A trade association of Mediterranean cruise **ports**. Its goal is to encourage cruise lines to call at or base ships in member ports. The association also fosters cooperation in other areas, such as security. Founded in June, 1996.

Medium-Speed Diesel
Diesel engine that normally operates from 250 to 1000 RPM and burns heavy fuel.

Meet and Greet
An airport service provided by cruise lines either directly or through a service company. This includes provision of greeters who stand at the gate, baggage claim area, or outside the customs area with a sign identifying the cruise line or ship. Passengers are helped with formalities, if any, and directed to vehicles that will transfer them to ship or hotel, the latter if a pre-cruise hotel stay has been booked. It is important to note that when a cruise line sells an **air/sea** package, it is the responsibility of the company to ensure that the passenger arrives at the ship prior to the ship's departure. Although a delay by an airline is not a cruise line's responsibility, it is still the cruise line's responsibility to get the passenger to the ship. If it has already sailed, the company makes arrangements for the passenger to join the ship at an early port of call – preferably the first! Since this service is often the passenger's first direct contact with the cruise line, it is an important one.

Messenger Line (Messenger Rope)

Megaship

Generally applied to **cruise ships** of 70,000 tons and larger. Within the last decade, megaships represent the convention of new ships being built for mass market companies. The first megaship is generally considered to have been Royal Caribbean's *Sovereign of the Seas*, 73,129 gross tons, built in 1987. It is interesting to note the extent to which these new **cruise ships** have changed the face of the passenger shipping industry. For twenty years after World War II, the world's largest liner was the original *Queen Elizabeth* of 1940, 83,673 gross tons, and sold by the original owners, Cunard, in 1968 and taken out of passenger service. Such legendary liners as the pre-war *Rex*, *Conte di Savoia*, *Bremen*, and *Europa* were all in the 50,000 ton range. Now, a **cruise ship** in excess of 70,000 tons is not unusual and those in excess of 100,000, while justly notable, are not unique. The reason why new **cruise ships** have such gigantic tonnage figures is that a **gross ton**, or **gross register ton** – is 100 cubic feet of space enclosed and the new cruise giantesses, designed for fair-weather sailing at fairly low speeds, can afford to be broad of beam. In contrast, a transatlantic liner such as *France*, now NCL's *Norway*, had to be long and lean in order to maintain a demanding schedule in all weather. A comparison of *Norway's* **hull** with that of new **cruise ships** is instructive in this respect.

Memorandum

A comment made by a classification society inspector about a deficiency in a ship that does not compromise seaworthiness. A notation is made together with a timetable for correction. In some cases, the item may remain pending forever but is subject to periodic inspection.

Memorandum of Understanding

See **Letter of Intent.**

Messenger Line (Messenger Rope)

A relatively thin rope, attached to the ship's major mooring line, thrown by an arriving ship's crew to the **linemen** on the pier. The latter use the messenger rope to haul the heavy mooring line, or

hawser, onto the pier so that it can be secured to a **bollard**, holding the ship to the wharf. This process is repeated both fore and aft until the ship can be hauled sufficiently close to the pier that supplemental **mooring lines** can be dropped directly to the pier's surface.

Messenger Rope
See **Messenger Line**.

Messing Charge
Charge to an on-board concessionaire for food provided to their staff on board.

Metacentric Height
See **Stability**.

MHA
See **Marine Hotel Association (MHA)**.

Mid-Size Vessel
A mid-sized **cruise ship** is now considered to be one in the 50,000-ton range, though interpretations here may vary. In the 1920-1970 era, the average size of vessel was 22,000 tons. This was large enough to provide all the comforts of ocean travel, to provide a speed of slightly more than twenty knots, and to keep the **draft** to 28.5 feet. Within this limitation, one could build a ship that could maintain a North Atlantic schedule in a variety of weathers with reasonable comfort and call at warm-water ports popular with cruise passengers.

Midships Section
See **Structural Cross Section**.

Monkey Island
Traditional open area above a ship's **wheelhouse**. Since this frequently contains communications equipment and a compass, this deck is frequently closed to passengers. Many modern **cruise ships** have such facilities as observation bars and **cabins** on decks above the **bridge**. Hence, a monkey island is no longer a universal feature in passenger ship design.

Monkey's Fist
Knot in the end of a **line** sometimes used to make it easier to throw a line onto a pier as a ship docks. The line is then grabbed by the **lineman**, the major

hawser is dragged onto the pier, and the vessel's **lines** are made fast to the **bollard** on the pier.

Mooring Buoy
A floating buoy attached to the **harbor** or ocean bottom by means of a chain or wire.

Mooring Deck
A deck area in the **bow** or **stern** of a ship containing mooring **hawsers**, winches, and other items used for securing a vessel to a pier. In ocean **liners**, both areas were usually open to the sky in bow or stern. In giant new **cruise ships**, the mooring deck is often a small, mostly enclosed area with only a small lateral opening through which ropes are passed. This keeps the shipboard end of the hawser closer to pier level, facilitating the mooring process and rendering it more secure.

Mooring Line
A thick rope used to secure a ship to the wharf. Also referred to frequently as a **hawser**, which defines the rope itself, not to its use.

Mortgage Interest Insurance
Often required by a mortgagee for protection from loss in the event that an insurance company does not pay because of negligent operation of a vessel.

Motor Vessel (MV)
A diesel-engined ship. Also referred to as motor ship, in which case the prefix M.S. is used rather than M.V. The two prefixes are, however, synonymous.

Moulded Depth
Distance between the top of the bottom-most plate to the top of the **hull**.

MPCU
See **Marine Pollution Control Unit**.

MPWMS
See **Multi Purpose Waste Management System**.

Mr. "D" Count
All **cruise ships**, prior to entering a United States port, must advise the Public Health Service of the number of cases of diarrhea that have occurred on board during the cruise. The report is forwarded via the office of the line. This obscure label is used to avoid calling attention to the count.

MS

See **Motor Vessel**.

MSA

See **Marine Safety Agency**.

Multi Purpose Waste Management System (MPWMS)

Beginning in the early 1990's, the cruise industry began to recycle and process its trash and garbage. Before then, garbage was never an issue. It was either removed from the vessel in **port** at low cost or disposed of, in terms of today's ethics, in an environmentally unsound manner. See also **Wider Caribbean Initiative for Cruise Ship-Generated Waste (WCISW)**. Today, **cruise ships** are equipped with sophisticated MPWMS that allows for the processing and storing of solid waste. Aluminum, glass, and cardboard are being recycled and in some cases sold, much as on land.

Multi-Deck Showrooms

The main show lounge on a vessel that can rise two or more decks. For reasons of traffic flow, these are usually located in the **bow** or **stern**. In ocean liners used as **cruise ships**, the First Class or Main Lounge most often doubled as a showroom. It was often two or more decks high but, other than a bandstand, had no equipment that supported production shows. As the cruise industry matured, entertainment became an increasingly competitive area among cruise lines. Aboard the 101,000-ton *Carnival Destiny*, the showroom itself is three full decks high, but such other features as a band pit and overhead space to house lighting and backdrops increase the vertical penetration to as much as five decks.

Multiday Cruises

While this term is self-descriptive as applying to cruises of at least overnight duration, it is an important factor in analyzing cruise passenger figures issued by various **ports** and segments of the cruise industry. The breakdown between multiday and day cruises is required to place in perspective the performance of any cruise **terminal port** or port of call.

Muster Station

Point where passengers in a given section of the accommodation are to go in the event of an emergency. This may or may not be adjacent to **lifeboats** on the open **deck**. A muster station can be a designated part of a public room.

MV
See **Motor Vessel.**

N

NACOA
See **National Association of Cruise-Oriented Agencies.**

Naming Ceremony
See **Christening or Naming Ceremony**

National Accounts.
Large travel companies with national distribution of travel products. Individual offices are either fully owned e.g. American Express, a franchise operation, or consortia. These accounts typically receive commission **overrides** and other benefits in return for high levels of sales.

National Association of Cruise-Oriented Agencies (NACOA)
A non-profit trade association of members specializing in selling cruises. Founded in 1985 to address the needs and concerns of agencies in this category, and for networking.

National Transportation Safety Board (NTSB)
Best known for its role in investigating the cause of airplane accidents, NTSB also has jurisdiction over **cruise ships** in U.S. ports or in coastal waters; also, over U.S. **cruise ships** wherever they sail. This is an independent U.S. governmental agency charged by Congress with investigating civil aviation accidents and significant accidents involving other forms of transportation. Rules of NTSB are found in Chapter VIII, Title 49, of the U.S. Code. Although it has no regulatory or enforcement power, the impartiality and thoroughness with which investigations are conducted give it great credibility and indirect power. Founded in 1967, it is available around the clock to go into action when an accident under its jurisdiction occurs. It is also the NTSB's responsi-

Nautical Expenses

bility to submit recommendations about transportation safety to the Secretary of Transportation for consideration and implementation.

Nautical Expenses

Deck department expenses that support getting the ship from point "a" to point "b". These relate to such items as navigational equipment, rope, charts, weather reports, etc.

Nautical Mile

A unit of measurement for distances at sea. One nautical mile = 6,080 feet. In measuring speed, one nautical mile per hour = one **knot** or 1.15 miles per hour. A nautical mile is equal to one minute of latitude on the earth's surface. Since the earth is not precisely round, this unit of measurement is actually greater in length near the poles than at the equator. The average length of a nautical mile, taking into consideration this variance, is 6,077 feet. The 6,080 figure is achieved by rounding upward.

Naval Architect

One who designs ships. Many cruise lines have their own team of naval architects who supervise the design of the line's vessels in cooperation with the shipyard. Commonly, they also serve as the owners' representative in managing the construction process.

Navigation

The process of safely moving a vessel from one place to another. With satellite technology and **global positioning systems**, navigation has become more of a science and slightly less of an art than in ancient days when navigators relied solely on the position of the sun and stars.

Nearby Foreign Port

Coastwise shipping laws, as outlined in the Passenger Services Act of 1886, make it a violation of law to transport cruise passengers from one U.S. port to another without calling at a **"distant foreign port."** Distant foreign ports include all those not bearing the designation "nearby foreign

Net Yield

port." The latter include any foreign port in North America, Central America, and the Bermuda Islands, or the West Indies (including the Bahama Islands, but not including the Leeward Islands of the Netherlands Antilles, i.e., Aruba, Bonaire, and Curacao). A port in the U.S. Virgin Islands is considered a nearby foreign port.

Net Airfare
Airfare that is net of any commission. When provided by the cruise line, it is negotiated on a wholesale basis with the airline. Where commissions are paid to travel agents, the commissions are underwritten by the cruise line and added to the "net airfare" figure.

Net On-Board Revenue
Net profit from on-board sales in bars, casino, shops, beauty salon, etc. for a given ship or company.

Net Per Diem
Actual revenue from cruise ticket sales less discounts, expenses for travel agent commissions, passenger transfers to and from the ship, airfare when purchased through the cruise line – divided by **passenger cruise days**.

Net Sea Revenue (NSR)
All revenues a **cruise ship** generates including ticket sales, on-board revenues, shore excursions, and all other vessel-related income.

Net Tonnage
Like a **gross ton,** a net ton is equal to a hundred cubic feet of space enclosed. However, only revenue space is included in net tonnage figures. In a cargo ship, this represents cubic cargo capacity. In a **cruise ship,** this includes passenger accommodation but not crew quarters, **machinery space,** the **bridge,** etc.

Net Win
Profit from a casino, or machine or table within a casino. Here, "win" represents the cruise line perspective rather than that of the consumer.

Net Yield
See **Net Sea Revenue (NSR).**

Dictionary of the Cruise Industry

Newbuildings

Refers to ships that are either on order or are being constructed by a shipyard. The term commonly applies to a ship up until time of delivery. Use is especially common before a ship has been named.

Niche Operator

A cruise line, generally a small one, offering a specialized cruise product. The niche, or specialization, may be based on itinerary, type of ship, or type of cruise experience. Some examples: Society Expeditions, offering soft adventure cruises; Swan's Hellenic Cruises, specializing in on-board lectures and scholarly interests in shore excursions; and World Explorer Cruises which also caters to those looking for a learning as well as a cruise experience.

Niche Player

Slang term for **niche operator.**

No Sale Status

(1) Where a travel agent or a chain of travel agents declares that they will not sell the product of a specific cruise line; (2) where a cruise line will not accept bookings from an agent or agent organization. In the first case, it can be an act of reprisal i.e. they have not received the commission levels desired from that cruise line; or, they have signed an agreement with another cruise line that they wouldn't sell any other product. In (2), a cruise line may define a travel agent as a no sale because they have caught that agent or one of a chain of agents rebating part of the sales commission to a customer. Cruise lines strongly discourage rebating, preferring to set the lowest cruise price level themselves. Instead of refunding commissions to customers, cruise lines prefer that the money be used in support of general sales efforts, to maintain a robust agent community, and to encourage agents to sell cruises rather than other types of vacations which often pay less commission to agents.

No Tipping Required Policy

See **Tipping Policies.**

Non-potable Fresh Water

Fresh water used other than for drinking and functions requiring drinking-water standards (see **Potable Water**). Examples: engine room, laundry, waste treatment, and washing decks (except in a ship's medical facility, where potable standards are required). Also called technical water.

Noncallable Loan

That part of a debt which cannot be called by a bank. This is a feature of "strong" loans that can finance the future of a company through good times and bad. **Callable** loans are "weak" loans that may be recalled when a company most needs them.

Noncombustible Material

A material that does not burn or give off flammable vapors in sufficient quantity to ignite at temperatures up to 750 degrees centigrade. **SOLAS** requires that all materials used in the construction of **bulkheads**, ceilings, and linings must meet this standard beginning in 2005. All existing ships will have to comply by 2010. The implication of this is that all vessels not constructed to SOLAS 1974 standards will require massive, and uneconomic, conversion.

Normal Crew

The amount of **crew** assigned to a vessel under normal operations and itinerary. This number is usually listed on the company's brochure as well as in guide books. The normal crew may be different from the actual crew on a given sailing depending on the number of passengers and the type of entertainment scheduled. Where ships stay full the year 'round, and where operation is fairly standardized e.g. in the mass market, the normal crew is generally the same as the actual crew on board.

Normal Operational and Habitable Condition

A **SOLAS** term for the condition where normal operational conditions obtain in the ship as a whole, including "…machinery, services, means and aids ensuring propulsion, ability to steer, safe navigation, fire and flooding safety, internal and external communication and signals, means of escape, and emergency boat winches, as well as the designed comfortable conditions of habitability…"

Norwegian Form
See **Barecon**.

Not Under Command (NUC)
A disabled ship not able to control direction or actions. To minimize the chance of collision, this status must be communicated according to the provisions of the **IMO** International Regulations for Preventing Collisions at Sea.

NSR
See **Net Sea Revenue**.

NTSB
See **National Transportation Safety Board**.

NUC
See **Not Under Command**.

Nuclear Power (as Means of Propulsion)
The first nuclear passenger vessel, actually a **combi-liner**, was the American *Savannah*, 13,599 gross tons, sixty passengers, and built in 1961. Operated initially by States Marine Lines, it actually carried passengers between American and Mediterranean ports in 1964-65 following a series of initial demonstration voyages. Taken over by American Export in 1965, it continued to sail as a cargo ship without passengers until **laid up** in January, 1972. The only nuclear powered ship to currently offer cruises is the Russian icebreaker *Sovetskiy Soyuz*. The vessel has offered adventure cruises since 1991 carrying a hundred passengers supported by one hundred fifty staff. Among the itineraries: a cruise to the North Pole. Two nuclear reactors provide steam for two turbines powering six generators providing a speed of 19.5 knots. Draft is thirty-nine feet, limiting worldwide deployments.

O

Obstructed View, Cabin With
Term commonly used to describe an outside **cabin** where the view of the sea is obstructed – generally by lifeboats, related equipment, or deck structures. Frequently, cabins are described as "obstructed view" in brochures where this condition is present. Obstructions can be slight or

Oily Water Separator

almost total. Where lifeboats are carried in recesses within a ship's superstructure, a number of cabins are likely to have obstructed views. Generally, cabins with obstructed views command lower rates than those where view is unrestricted.

Occupancy
Passenger Cruise Days divided by the number of **lower berth days**; expressed as a percentage.

Ocean Liner
See **Liner**

Off Hire
When a ship, normally operating under charter, for the time being does not fulfil the charter conditions set forth in the **charter party**, thereby enabling the charterer not to pay hire.

Officer of the Watch
Officer in charge of the bridge and, therefore, of the ship at any given time. Of course, the **captain** is summoned and takes over direction of the ship if any potentially problematic situation develops such as major traffic, unusual weather, or other phenomenon.

Official Number
See **Ship Identification Number.**

Oil Record Book
This documents oil pollution control measures aboard a **cruise ship**. It lists oil taken on board, oil used or properly disposed of, and oil remaining on board (ROB) plus engine sludge. If these figures don't account for all oil taken on board, the port state control inspectors will want to know where the "missing" oil has gone.

Oil/Water Separator
See **Oily Water Separator.**

Oily Water Separator
A centrifuge or other device used to separate oil from water in a bilge or other space first used to store oil and then salt water ballast so that the latter can be discharged into the ocean and the former transported for environmentally acceptable disposal. This is extremely useful where a **void** has been used both to hold salt water ballast and to

store fuel oil, or in other situations where water has become contaminated.

On-board Product
The type and quality of cruise experience provided on a given **cruise ship** or line. This general term includes facilities, cuisine, service, and basic style of cruising. Style can be interpreted to include such diverse items as standards of dress, age of passengers, and the type of entertainment provided.

On-hire, Off-hire Survey
Surveys undertaken to certify a vessel's condition that are part of a charter agreement. The on-hire survey is done on the owner's time and the off-hire on the charterer's time. In many cases, the owner and charterer will decide on a joint survey in which the cost is shared. These surveys reveal the condition of the vessel on **delivery** versus **redelivery** in order to establish the need for repairs and any necessary compensation from the charterer to the owner.

Open Jaw
When a cruise starts in one country and ends in another, usually because of **cabotage** restrictions. Also applies to two **ports** in the same country provided the vessel flies the flag of that nation.

Open Sitting (Dining Room)
On most ships, passengers are assigned to either first or second sitting for dining room meals. However, when a ship is in **port**, or on some lines for breakfast and/or lunch, passengers may appear for their meal at any point within a stated period of time, e.g. 7 - 9 a.m. for breakfast and 12 - 2 p.m. for lunch. The same arrangement is at times announced for dinner when there are excursions returning late so that those normally assigned to first sitting would return to the ship too late to dine at the normal time. The advantage of open sitting is flexibility for the passenger. The disadvantages are that guests frequently dine away from their accustomed dining room waiters and service at times suffers; and adverse weather can cause an unexpectedly high number of passengers to dine on board rather than ashore if the ship is in port, causing lines and presenting a challenge to staff.

Operating Ratio
Compares a cruise line's operating expenses with gross income.

Ordinary Seaman (OS)
Seaman with some experience but who has not yet qualified for the designation of **Able-bodied Seaman (AB)**.

Out Island
See **Private Island**.

Out-of-the-Way Ports of Call
Specific operational meaning: a **port** requiring major deviation from an existing itinerary and courses dictated by it.

Outboard
Toward the side of a ship; away from the center; indicates a direction or relative location.

Outside Cabin
See **Cabin**.

Outsourcing
Just as with many land-based companies, many cruise lines subcontract for such functions as food and/or bar service, retail shops, photography service, and even **port** talks. A few lines even subcontract for **deck and engine** services.

Over-all
When applied to dimensions, the term means total, including any incidental structure that may extend the particular dimension.

Over-Capacity
More tonnage on a particular trade route than demand. This traditional term became a much-used one in the late eighties when the first wave of **megaships** were ordered and began coming into service. Industry skeptics questioned the feasibility of filling the additional **berths**. Now that it is clear that the new ships have generated additional business at least equal to their capacity, the term has fallen into disuse. The efficiency of the new megaships has also kept fares low, something that has contributed to the continuing high demand for cruise vacations. It would take a dramatic economic downturn to change this situation.

Overlap (Turnover)

When one **Master** (Captain) relieves another, the two will sail on the same ship for a week or more as a step in familiarizing the new Captain.

Override

Payment of greater than the standard commission by a cruise line to a travel agent in consideration, generally, of business volume accorded to the cruise line.

Owner's Suite

A tradition of the shipping industry, special accommodation designed for owners and guests is and has often been provided. Such accommodation is used for cruise line executives, by especially productive travel agents, or major organizers of groups. Sometimes, the best suites now bear this name and are available for sale to the public. However, more traditional was the owner's suite aboard Carnival Cruise Line's *Carnivale*, built into what had been the first class Sun Lounge when the ship sailed as *Empress of Britain*, and used by the owner and guests. During the ship's final few years with Carnival, the space served as a children's playroom.

P

P & I Club

See **Protection and Indemnity Club**.

Panama Canal Tonnage Certificate

Panama Canal fees are assessed on the basis of a tonnage different from a vessel's other tonnage measurements. This Certificate, indicating the tonnage on which Panama Canal fees are to be based, is issued by a ship's flag **administration** or **classification society**.

Panamax

Size standard that equals the largest ship dimensions compatible with Panama Canal transit. See also **beam**.

Panting
When, under pressure (as in a heavy sea), **hull plates** bend in and out as pressure increases and recedes.

Part-Ship Charter
See **Partial Charter.**

Partial Charter (Part-Ship Charter)
Most companies make a distinction between large groups and situations where thirty to forty per cent of passengers on a cruise are part of one group. At this point, the group becomes a part-ship charter, with different rules for payment and confirmation so that the cruise line is protected and is guaranteed to receive revenues from the firm part-chartering the vessel. A significant challenge with such cruises is to ensure that the individually-booked passengers on board have a pleasant vacation experience and are not made to feel that they have been excluded from a major part of that cruise's attractions. At the same time, on a very large ship, the charterer and the line have the opportunity to arrange for major entertainment flown to the ship especially for the group which can be provided in major lounges at times when they are not normally in use. Special information desks can also provide a variety of services for the "partial charter" booked.

Partial Transit
Generally applied to cruises that partially traverse the Panama Canal, almost always from the Caribbean side, generally sailing into Gatun Lake and then returning to the Caribbean. This makes it feasible to give passengers many of the experiences of a Transcanal Cruise on a Caribbean itinerary. It also makes it possible to provide this within a seven-day cruise originating in Jamaica, Aruba, or at some other Caribbean port. The partial transit is also used on longer Caribbean cruises of ten days or more. It is a dramatic "value added" to a Caribbean itinerary. For the round-trip transit from the Caribbean to Gatun Lake and return, cruise lines pay the normal one-way toll for a complete transit.

Passage Contract

Cruise ticket, called a contract because it outlines extensively the conditions of passage including limitations of responsibility on the part of the cruise line.

Passed Around

Used to describe vessels that have changed hands several times. It is normally used for vessels that have changed names at least two or three times, though there are some vessels that have sailed under a half dozen names and managements. Two of the best examples of "passed around" are the ships built as Moore McCormack Line's *Argentina* and *Brasil* in 1958 which have been operated under seven and eight different names respectively. They are still in service under the ownership of Commodore Cruise Lines as the **Enchanted Isle** and **Universe Explorer** (*Enchanted Seas of Commodore* operated under charter by World Explorer Cruises). In spite of this questionable distinction, they are excellent and soundly constructed examples of the American shipbuilder's art of the Fifties, designed with many defence features to suit them as troopships in time of war. Unfortunately, these same features made them rather expensive to operate.

Passenger Boarding Bridge

In a seaport or airport, designed to allow passengers to pass between terminal and ship or airplane without exposure to weather. This tends to be more complex with **cruise ships** than with airplanes. With aircraft doors, height variances are relatively small. On Carnival Cruise Lines alone, these vary from nine to forty-seven feet. The differences are accentuated further by tides. Providing adequately for these variances is both complicated and expensive.

Passenger Cargo Ship

See **Combivessel**.

Passenger Cruise Day (PCD)

A term used to describe one of the basic cruise units. One person staying on a ship for one night equals one PCD. A couple on a seven day cruise is equal to fourteen PCD's. The unit is the basis for budgeting, pricing, cost control, cost accounting , and other reporting. The term "guest cruise day" is

Passenger Services Act (PSA)

also sometimes used, denoting that ships are no longer just for transportation but in the hospitality business as well.

Passenger Facility Charge
Fee charged by port authority for use of a terminal.

Passenger Profile
Demographic aspects of passengers on a ship, line, itinerary, or for the industry as a whole. This includes such factors as income and educational level, age, family status, language(s) spoken, and country of national origin. The profile is one factor in planning a cruise experience that is likely to appeal to clientele.

Passenger Services Act (PSA)
The Passenger Services Act is Title 46 of the U.S. Code, Section 282, and was proposed and passed by Congress in 1886. It regulates the transportation of U.S. or non-U.S. passengers and prevents foreign flagged vessels from carrying passengers between U.S. **ports**. It allows voyages from the United States to foreign ports, or cruises sailing from and returning to the same port provided that passengers both **embark** and **disembark** in that same port. It also allows for voyages to nowhere with continuous movement that go beyond the three-mile limit and start as well as end in the same U.S. port. A ship on a cruise from a United States port can call at another U.S. port only if the vessel is undertaking an international cruise and calling at a **"distant foreign port."** Many ports in nearby areas have been designated as **"nearby foreign ports"** and therefore don't qualify. For example, a cruise from Fort Lauderdale via Cozumel and the Panama Canal to Los Angeles will not qualify, because it touches only at a Mexican port which is not considered a distant foreign port. This is why cruise companies are adding either Aruba or Cartegena to their itineraries in order to undertake **Transcanal** cruises between two U.S. ports. Another eccentricity of this legislation: the *Carnival Destiny* itinerary that actually calls at three U.S. ports – Puerto Rico, Saint Croix, and St Thomas is exempt because San Juan is not regarded as a U.S. Port. The U.S. Customs Services is charged with implementing the Act. The

penalty imposed for unlawful transportation of passengers between coastwise points is $200 for each passenger transported and landed. The PSA is sometimes mistakenly referred to as the Jones Act. However, the latter law does not relate to passengers but to freight.

Passenger Ship

A vessel that carries more than twelve passengers. This definition is used by **SOLAS** and by the industry in general.

Passenger Ship Safety Certificate

Form provided by flag administration or classification society certifying the safety of an individual passenger ship based on compliance with **IMO** regulations.

Passenger Shipping Association (PSA)

Trade association for cruise and ferry companies operating from UK. Also known as Ocean Travel Development. Formed in 1958, the year when the number of transatlantic passengers by air first exceeded those travelling by sea, its initial message was promoting ocean travel as a vacation choice rather than as a means of transportation. The Association now divides its resources between the cruise and ferry sectors of ocean travel in UK. Historically, the association helped a number of major companies, such as P & O, survive the transition from passenger line voyages to cruising at a time when these lines were saddled by a great deal of uneconomic and unsuitable tonnage.

Passenger Space Ratio

Gross tonnage divided by number of passengers. This measure is often equated to the amount of space on board for passengers. While this literally is a measure of passenger space, it may or may not be reflected in passenger impressions regarding the total space since it includes cabins and purely operational areas. In theory, a ship could have very few public rooms and almost no deck space and still have a very satisfactory passenger-space ratio. Space ratios do tend to vary more than the standard of accommodation generally. While one would expect a first-generation purpose-built **cruise ship** like the *Olympic Countess* (formerly, *Cunard Countess*) to have a space ratio of 21.4, Carnival's mass-market *Paradise* has a relatively high space ratio of 34; that of *Rotterdam VI* is 46.9; and the ultra-luxury *Seabourn Pride*, 47

Passenger Spaces
Spaces provided for the direct accommodation of passengers. **SOLAS** includes in this definition baggage, stores, provision and mail rooms in addition to the passenger accommodation.

Passenger Vessel Operator (PVO)
Legal term used by the **Federal Maritime Commission (FMC)** when referring to commercial watercraft that carry passengers. Of course, cruise lines are included in this category.

Passthrough Revenues
Those revenues that do not contribute to profitability of a company. The best example of **passthrough revenues** are airline tickets that are generally charged back to passengers at or near cost. Revenue that contributes to profitability is referred to as decoupling revenue.

Pax
Abbreviation for passengers.

PCD
See **Passenger Cruise Day.**

Peaks
Ballast tanks or voids **fore** and **aft** low in the ship. The name comes from their unique shape dictated by curves in the **hull**.

Penalty Clause
In the cruise industry, most commonly applied to shipbuilding, ship repair, and vessel conversion. This involves a set sum of money due the shipowner if a vessel is delivered late, or fails to meet specifications in some important aspect e.g. to make its designed speed. Under such circumstances, the fine may either be paid or negotiated in return for other concessions.

Per Diem
Fare per day per passenger. This term is commonly-used by travel agents and consumers helpful to compare the fares of different cruise lines.

Per Person Per Day (PPD), Sales
Term, usually used in abbreviated form, denoting sales per person per day to describe on board revenues.

Perils of the Sea
Extreme and unpredictable weather conditions which result in loss or damage that ordinary skill and prudent navigation may not avoid.

Period of Roll
Time required for a ship to complete a rolling cycle, i.e. to roll to one side, then to the opposite, and returning to the original position.

Permeability
Portion of a given space that can hold water. This is an element used by **SOLAS** in determining the behavior of a ship in partially-flooded condition.

Personal Lifesaving Appliances
Individual lifesaving equipment including lifebuoys, lifejackets, and immersion suits, provided as required by **SOLAS** regulations.

Pilot
A qualified navigator, and frequently a qualified **master**, authorized by a **port** to assist the captain in navigating a vessel into and out of the harbor. In most major ports, the use of pilots is mandatory. The pilot is very familiar with the channel(s), traffic, and currents in the harbor(s). In very difficult areas of navigation, such as coastal Alaska, local regulations require that the pilot stay on board for the entire voyage. However, the captain has responsibility for the ship at all times. The role of the pilot is advisory except when transiting the Panama Canal where the pilot exercises prime authority.

Pilot Boarding Area
See **Pilot Station.**

Pilot Ladder
Used by **pilot** to **disembark** a ship on departure and **embark** on arrival. Subject to detailed **SOLAS** regulations in design. Known colloquially as "Jacob's Ladder."

Pilot Station
A location at sea near the entrance to a port or

Podded Azimuthing Propulsors

channel where the pilot boards the vessel; also known as the **pilot** boarding area. A fixed set of coordinates are given for each pilot station. An example is the one for Port Canaveral: 1 n.m. southeast of Light Buoy #3. Lat. 28-20.7N; Long 080-30.5W.

Pilotage
Fee assessed for the services of a **pilot**.

Piracy
The act of unlawfully attacking or seizing a ship on the high seas. The term is applied to those who raid ships in peacetime for financial gain though piracy can, of course, occur during wartime. Pirates are still a problem that must be guarded against in some areas, notably in Southeast Asia.

Pitch
(1) Motion created when a ship sails at right angles to swells resulting in a vertical motion of the **bow**. In a pitching motion, a passenger vessel tends to pivot at a point two-thirds of the way **aft**; (2) angle of a **propeller** blade at any given time. Most **cruise ships** use variable-pitch propellers that control both the speed and the direction of a vessel, avoiding the need to reverse engines or to vary engine speed.

Plimsoll Line (Plimsoll Mark)
Named after Samuel Plimsoll, member of the British Parliament and advocate for seamen's rights. Shows the maximum draft to which a ship may be loaded under five different sea conditions ranging from tropical fresh water to winter North Atlantic. The need for such a measure arose from a practice prevalent in the Nineteenth Century of overloading ships and compromising safety. Nowadays, every ship, passenger and cargo, must have such a mark with the abbreviated name of the vessel's **classification society** also given.

Podded Azimuthing Propulsors
Electric motors mounted in pods in place of, and in the approximate location of, **propellers** and **rudders**. These are of three types: tractor (where the propeller pulls the vessel); pusher, where the propeller is mounted behind the pod and exerts a

pushing action; and tandem, where two propellers are mounted on the pod, one fore and one aft, both turning in the same direction. Fixed-pitch propellers are generally used. This mode of propulsion was originated by the partnership Kvaerner Masa-Yards and ABB, though initial research and development was carried out at the Krylov Shipbuilding and Research Institute in St. Petersburg, Russia. Brand name for this version is Azipod. The Azipod is present in a major **cruise ship** for the first time as a feature Carnival's 70,400 gross-ton *Elation*. This ship and *Paradise* use a two-pod design. Royal Caribbean's 130,000 ton Project Eagle ships will each be equipped with three Azipods. Rival designs are being offered by Siemens-Propulsor which employs two propellers turning in the same direction and by others. Pods, as they are known, can turn in a 360-degree rotation, thus eliminating the need for a rudder. Advantages: 5-7% more hydrodynamically efficient, the savings variable depending on over-all ship design; less space required for propulsion units within the **hull**; superior steering capability; excellent reversing power; low noise and vibration since the water dampens these; and financial savings resulting from being ordered later in the construction process than conventionally-mounted electric motors.

Pods
See **Podded Azimuthing Propulsors.**

Points of Sale
Used to discuss the number of points of sale (places where cash or credit cards are accepted) vs. revenue, number of passengers, size of vessel, etc. The on board revenue per point of sale is an obvious factor in both efficiency and level of business.

Pooled Tipping
See **Tipping Policies.**

Port Briefing (Port Talk)

Poop Deck

In a traditional vessel, the deck furthest **aft** and highest. However, aboard modern **cruise ships**, what would normally be the poop deck is occupied by built-up **superstructure**, usually including a lido deck and pool. While quaint, the term has no real meaning with reference to a modern passenger ship.

Port

(1) A protected harbor with facilities for supporting ship operations, usually including an industrial zone or town/city, where a vessel may enter to load and unload passengers or cargo; (2) the left side of the ship when one faces the **bow**; (3) door or window between the inside and outside aboard ship. When applied to a door, it is usually an opening in the **hull**.

Port Agent

A person or a company that acts on behalf of a ship at a port of call. The agent represents the cruise line to local authorities including customs, immigration, public health, and the port authority. The port agent is involved in the clearance of the vessel, provisioning, stevedoring services, and assists the **Captain** in matters related to purchasing, transfer of **crew** members to and from airports, and arranging for the exact **berth** the vessel occupies. In recent years, port agents have also become involved with arranging shore excursions for passengers. Payment for core services is usually on the basis of a fixed fee per call, at times negotiated for a season, year, or for a fleet. Special services, such as emergency purchases, or actually providing transfer of crew or passengers to or from an airport are generally at extra cost.

Port Authority

Governing and administrative authority of a **port**; often, of an airport as well. The port authority handles day-to-day administrative operations, planning, and long-range policy issues. It is both a governing authority and a bureaucracy.

Port Briefing (Port Talk)

Briefing conducted on board by a member of the cruise staff providing information on one or more ports of call to passengers. The briefing includes information about shore excursions, shopping opportunities, customs and immigration information as well as **disembarkation** plans and security notices. In some instances, the port briefing also recommends local merchants who, in cooperative relationships with the cruise line, agree to guarantee merchandise and services. This provides additional income for cruise lines inasmuch as resulting sales are commissioned.

Port Captain

Position in the marine operations office of a cruise line. Provides general assistance to ship captains and officers in a variety of areas. These include information on **ports** including local regulations and unusual navigational conditions, special purchases, charts and other special assistance. Assists marketing department with itinerary planning. Frequently, this position is occupied by a retired captain.

Port Charges

These include special costs, such as head taxes imposed by local governments and routine operating expenses such as **dockage**, fees for the **harbor master** and **lineman**, sanitation fee, charges for customs and immigration, **pilot**, tug boats, **port agents**, and other items.

Port Control

A control point for marine traffic, generally used in large, busy harbors.

Port Disbursement Account

Invoice to a cruise line tendered by the line's **port agent**. All vendor invoices, such as those for customs, immigration, linesmen, **dockage** fees, etc., are normally included and attached.

Port of Entry

Initial port of call by a ship in a country where customs formalities must be undertaken.

Port of Registry

The **port** where the vessel is registered. The port of registry is normally one of the largest ports in the country and, according to international law, the port of registry must appear on the **stern** of the vessel just below the ship's name.

Port State Control

Inspection of a foreign vessel for compliance with **IMO** treaties including **SOLAS** and **MARPOL** when the ship first enters **port** in a country that is signatory to these international treaties. In the United States, these inspections are undertaken by the U.S. Coast Guard initially, before a vessel enters service from an American port, and then quarterly. All signatories are obligated to maintain this function, though not all have the resources to do a thorough job.

Port-to-Port Cruising

Term applied to an itinerary pattern where a ship begins a cruise in one **port** and terminates it at another, in contrast with the more common practice of returning to the same port. This is a popular pattern in **destination cruises**, and, except for Alaska, is most common outside North America and the Caribbean. Prime examples: Istanbul to Venice in the Mediterranean; Hong Kong to Singapore in the Far East; and Auckland, New Zealand to Sydney, Australia in the Antipodes. Also sometimes known as a one-way cruise or an **open jaw** itinerary.

Porthole

A round opening in the side of a ship. On lower **decks**, a steel covering called a **deadlight** is put in place when rough weather is anticipated. In the old days, especially before most passenger ships were air conditioned, portholes could be opened to admit fresh air. Portholes have now largely been replaced by larger square windows in most sections of most ships except where the location is directly at risk from large waves e.g. low and forward.

POSH

Synonym for luxurious or deluxe. Perhaps the leading theory concerning the origin of this term is as an acronym for "Port Out, Starboard Home," a designation stamped on the tickets of P & O passengers desiring a port-side cabin from England to destinations East of the Suez Canal, and starboard from the East back to Britain. Before the days of air conditioning, this arrangement assured passengers of a cabin on the shadier side of the ship throughout the round-trip and, therefore, more comfortable accommodation. Partridge's *Concise Dictionary of Slang and Unconventional English* indicates that the term may also be a corruption of *tosh*, a Scottish term meaning clean, neat, and trim; or a contraction of *polish*. But even Partridge admits that the P & O theory is the usual educated explanation and is plausible.

Positioning (or Repositioning) Cruises

Cruises operated not primarily because of their marketing desirability but to move a ship between **cruise areas**. Many of these are operated in the spring and fall as seasons change and ships are moved between climatic zones. Cruises that take or return a vessel to its normal service following **drydocking** or charter are normally referred to as repositioning cruises.

Post-Panamax

Refers to a generation of **cruise ships**, many still under construction, that have abandoned the **panamax** standard i.e. no attempt is made to conform to the limitations imposed by the Panama Canal. For the vessels in this category either completed or envisioned, the intent is to employ them exclusively in the Caribbean the year 'round, or in the Caribbean, Atlantic coastal waters, and the European area. The extreme economies of scale available in ships of more than 100,000 tons has prompted the move to abandon Panama Canal versatility in a selected number of ships and employ the panamax giantesses in appropriate markets not requiring passage through the Canal. First of these vessels was the *Carnival Destiny*; the second, *Grand Princess* of Princess Cruises. Royal Caribbean's Project Eagle ships of more than 136,000 tons continue the trend.

Potable Water

Fresh water that meets the standards required for drinking. According to the **Center for Disease Control**, this should be used for "...drinking, washing, bathing, showering; for use in the ship's hospital; for handling, preparing, or cooking food; and for cleaning storage and preparation areas, utensils, and equipment." This should meet the *International Standards for Drinking Water*, according

Prefabricated Construction

to CDC, "...especially the bacteriological, chemical, and physical requirements." References are from "Recommended Shipbuilding Construction Guidelines for Vessels Destined to Call on U.S. Ports" dated February 1, 1997.

Power Actuating System
Hydraulic equipment that controls the **rudder**. Includes steering gear power unit(s), rudder actuator, and related pipes/fittings.

Practique Certificate
Lifts short-term quarantine that has been placed on a ship; issued by Health Officer.

Pre - and Post Cruise Packages
This rather self-explanatory phrase is used to describe a one - or two - night hotel stay prior to or following a cruise, often combined with some touring arrangements. This is distinct from the **cruise and stay** concept involving longer stays at a shoreside hotel, or "cruise tour" which involves more extensive touring arrangements on land.

Pre-sold Shorex
Pre-sold shore excursions. The practice is common with groups, and may be included in the agreed-upon package price accorded to the travel agency, the "free shorex" serving as a sales incentive. Since the excursions are part of the financial deal, they are really in the pre-sold category. The term is also used for the situation where most or all shore excursions are included in the price of the cruise, a practice of Swan's Hellenic Cruises and some other operators.

Prefabricated Construction
The modern way of building **cruise ships**. Sections of a ship are built adjacent to the **dock** where the vessel itself is under construction. As each section is complete, it is hoisted and welded into place and becomes part of the ship. **Cabins** may be built in a factory far from the shipyard and transported to the yard for installation. This is in contrast to the era, as recently as the sixties, when each plate or piece of a ship was fashioned independently before being riveted or welded into place. This technique made possible the subtle curves characteristic of

the great liners that optimized their high-speed operation. If today's shipyards were dependent on such methods, it would not have been economically feasible to produce the cruise fleet of today.

Preferred Supplier

A series of arrangements between a travel agency and a cruise line/corporation whereby the agent is given incentives to steer the majority of bookings in a given category i.e. mass market, five-star luxury, or deluxe to one company or corporation. Incentives are generally in the form of commission **overrides**, priority access to space, and other special treatment. This is a particularly common practice with larger agency chains and consortia.

Premium Cruise Product

See **Premium Luxury Segment.**

Premium Segment

This is the segment that offers the finest accommodation, food and service available at sea, for Seabourn and Silversea at minimum fares as much as $900-$1000 per day per person, double. Inhabitants of this category include, in addition, Crystal and Radisson Seven Seas which offer somewhat lower fares. These smaller ships offer one-sitting dining; extremely spacious accommodation (except for *Song of Flower*, which excels in other ways), and highly personal service with standards of perfection not delivered in either deluxe or mass market. Crystal does not offer one-sitting dining, but presents the type of entertainment possible aboard larger ships along with other large-ship amenities. As with the **DeLuxe** category, there is no universal agreement on category labels or exactly which lines should be included within the segments.

Prepaid Tips

See **Tipping Policies.**

Pricing Pressure

Pressure to reduce fares in a weak market or in a situation of intense competition.

Private Auction

Where bids for the sale of a vessel are solicited from a select group of potential buyers.

Production Show

Private Company

Where ownership is in the hands of a few individuals or companies, and shares are not sold to the general public. Until the decade of the 1990's, most cruise lines were in this category. The pressure to raise money to build new, larger, and more efficient ships has created pressure for more and more companies to issue publicly-traded stock resulting in fewer and fewer privately-held cruise lines.

Private Island (Out Island) as Itinerary Feature

Initiated by NCL, first at Little San Salvador, then at Little Stirrup Cay in the Bahamas, the out island stop or private island as an itinerary feature is a beach party day where the ship anchors off the beach. Passengers enjoy the sea and sun, water sports, and increasingly elaborate facilities ashore such as shops and bars. These island stops have proven to be very popular with passengers, and more and more lines have been buying or leasing islands, or parts of islands, for this purpose. Another early effort was Odessa America's Shashlik parties ashore in Roatan Island from its *Odessa* in 1974. Since then, Holland America, Princess, Royal Caribbean, and Disney have provided such stops – the latter the first to actually have facilities for its ships to dock. Royal Caribbean has two: Great Stirrup Cay in the Bahamas (dubbed by the marketers "Coco Cay"), and Labadee Shores, a development on the coast of Haiti.

Product Line

(1) Collection of cruise **brands** owned by a single corporation; (2) different itineraries offered by a single cruise line; (3) varying levels of cruise product offered by a single cruise line, e.g. by the Cunard Line until recently.

Production Show

A specially-produced music and dance review produced for the entertainment program of a cruise line. Production is usually by a separate company that may or may not be owned by the line. These shows have become more common as **cruise ships** have increased in size and as the entertainment budget for each ship has grown larger. Production shows are now the centerpiece of entertainment aboard a number of cruise lines. Even those lines where the size of ship or physical surroundings don't permit the presentation of full reviews, smaller more modest versions are a fixture of on board entertainment. These entertainments have the advantage of transcending the language barrier and serving very well multinational and multilingual passenger lists.

Production Singer

A singer in a **production show** on board a vessel. This is in contrast with those who appear as part of cabaret acts, or as part of instrumental/vocal groups in individual public rooms.

Promenade Deck

(1) Partially shaded **deck**, often encircling the **superstructure**, at the midpoint of the ship as measured from **waterline** to top-most deck; (2) at times, the enclosed deck containing the principal public rooms. The latter became a feature of many post-war passenger ships with the rise of the practice of extending public rooms to the edge of the ship to make them larger. With the rise of complete airconditioning, and the bad weather prevalent on the North Atlantic, this practice made sense. It also tended to increase the amount of revenue-producing space. Walk-around (or wrap-around) outdoor mostly-shaded promenade decks are popular features with passengers who engage in weight control and general exercise by walking laps. Such features consume area that would otherwise be available as revenue space, but the sacrifice in revenue is considered to be worthwhile for what this feature brings to the cruise experience of many passengers. Aboard most classic Transatlantic liners, some or all of the promenade was glass enclosed to enable passengers to lounge in deck chairs even in cold or rainy weather. During the post-World War II era, especially aboard ships designed to cruise part of the year, this space became more and more of a public room with some of the promenade actually becoming part of

Protection and Indemnity Club (P & I Club)

certain public rooms e.g. the main lounge. The Queen's Room on *QE2* is an example of this. When the *France* became the **cruise ship** *Norway*, the first class enclosed promenade was converted into a boulevard-like cafe. Carnival Cruise Lines eliminated the practice of having this space on both sides of the ship and, beginning with *Holiday*, incorporated a slightly wider promenade on one side. The space, a feature of all subsequent CCL ships, is used much like those aboard *Norway* which extend completely around the vessel. While the indoor promenade still exists in some form aboard a number of **cruise ships,** it has been eliminated in others e.g. Holland America ships beginning with the new *Statendam*. However, its outdoor counterpart, sheltered from the sun but open to the breeze is a prized feature.

Propeller

A series of blades attached to a shaft that propel a ship through the water when rotated. The shaft connects the propeller either directly or indirectly to the engine(s).

Propulsion System

A ship's main engines that drive the ship forward or astern.

Protection and Indemnity Association

See **Protection and Indemnity Club (P & I Club)**.

Protection and Indemnity Club (P & I Club)

A mutual insurance association covering a variety of risks, some not convertible by other forms of insurance, such as damage to cargo. These "clubs" arose in Britain during the eighteenth century when shipowners were not satisfied with the extent of coverage available, or with its cost. Several owners, normally within a single geographic area, would band together and share insurance risks of the members. When these clubs were first established, **hull** insurance was available only from two companies: Royal Exchange Assurance and London Assurance, in addition to individuals operating from Lloyd's Coffee House. In 1824, the monopoly of these two companies was lifted and P & I clubs as originally conceived went into decline. However, with the rise of passenger travel and increase in shipping activity during the Nineteenth Century, proliferation of third-party claims created a need for the types of protection afforded by these clubs. Associations similar to the clubs were established and grew once again – this time, incorporated so that it is the club and not the individual shipowners that bears the risks. Currently, such insurance covers third party liability rather than the original hull insurance and other types of coverage. The clubs are "not for profit" mutual insurance companies that issue no shares nor pay dividends. Final cost to participants is dependent on the level of claims being experienced rather than on a fixed price for coverage.

Protection and Indemnity Insurance

The equivalent of liability insurance on land. Protection and Indemnity is the shipowner's liability insurance which is available through a world wide network of mutual insurance associations. See **Protection and Indemnity Club**. A feature of this coverage is absence of a fixed premium and in its place, a cost level that is dependent on the actual level of claims being experienced.

Protocol of 1996 to the Merchant Shipping (Minimum Standards) Convention, 1976 (No. 147)

See **International Labor Organization (ILO) Maritime Conference**.

Protocol of Delivery

A document covering the delivery process for a new ship from shipyard to owner; for an older ship, from owner to owner; or for a ship, terminating or beginning a charter, between charterer and owner. Includes all the documents and certificates that accompany delivery, such as change-of-command documentation and certificate of inventories.

Protrusion

Narrow extension of part of a vessel beyond the **beam**, frequently **bridge wings** or at pool deck level. This condition is of significance for **cruise ships** transiting the Panama Canal. Those with protrusions qualify for only a temporary permit that allows occasional use of the Canal. The fear is damage to the canal locks as well as adjoining buildings and equipment.

Provision Master

A petty officer on board the vessel who has the responsibility of issuing food and beverages to departments aboard ship. Responsibilities vary from one cruise line to another. On some ships, the Provision Master's responsibilities are vast and include food purchasing in various **ports** as well as disbursement of all consumable goods (i.e, toilet paper, dishes, etc.). In other companies, the Provision Master is not engaged in purchasing but only in distribution.

PSA

See **Passenger Services Act (PSA)**.

PSR

See **Passenger Space Ratio**.

Public Health

See **Center for Disease Control**.

Public Spaces

Defined by **SOLAS** to include halls, dining rooms, lounges, and similar spaces that are permanently enclosed. This definition reflects general usage.

Purser

Traditionally, the officer in charge of handling all financial affairs aboard ship. Over-time, duties evolved into the hotel area to the point that the Purser frequently has had senior hotel managerial responsibility. Sometimes, there is also a crew purser. Inevitably, responsibilities and position titles vary from line to line.

PVO

See **Passenger Vessel Operator**.

Quad Share

A cabin sold to four individuals (same sex, over the age of eighteen) who are not travelling together.

Quarter

Direction from **amidships** of forty-five degrees on either side of directly **astern**.

Quartermaster

Quartermaster
A sailor on a vessel who has the responsibility to steer as directed by the officer of the watch. In today's modern **cruise ships** where vessels usually operate on automatic pilot, the quartermaster still steers manually in harbors and in close proximity to other vessels. He also assists the officer of the watch in various navigational duties.

Quay
Pier or **dock** where a **cruise ship** is **berthed**. Frequently extended to mean the area immediately around the dock.

Quayside
See **Quay**.

R

R.O.
See **Reverse Osmosis**.

Rail Program
The rail counterpart of **air/sea**, popular in Europe and in some areas of North America. Can be part of a special group arrangement.

Raked
To increase the impression of speed and grace, funnels and masts of many ships – old and new – lean back with the top further aft than the bottom. This also has aerodynamic benefit.

RAM
Restricted ability maneuver. Used when a vessel's capability of maneuvering is restricted by a legitimate activity. RAM status is signaled by special lights at night and signals hoisted aloft by day. It bestows certain right-of-way privileges when meeting other ships.

Rat Guard
Metal disk, with hole in center, placed on mooring **hausers** to prevent the passage of rats from the pier to the ship.

Ratings
Non-officer personnel in the **deck and engine** departments.

Ratio of Staff to Passengers
See **Passenger Space Ratio**.

Readily Accessible
Area or equipment used in food handling that the Center for Disease Control defines as "Exposed or capable of being exposed for cleaning or inspection without the use of tools." (ref: CDC Construction Guidelines, 1/9/97).

Rebate
Applied to cruise industry marketing, when a travel agency gives to the consumer part of the commissioned earned. This is discouraged by the cruise industry as undermining the distribution system – the network of travel agencies on which cruise lines depend for most sales. It would be preferable, for instance, for an agency to invest the money in staff training or higher salaries to enhance agent skills and reduce turnover.

Recruitment and Placement of Seafarers Convention, 1996 (No. 179)
See **International Labor Organization (ILO) Maritime Conference**.

Redelivery
The process whereby a charterer returns a vessel to the owner as called for in the charter agreement.

Refit
Traditional maritime term for refurbishing. May be applied to work on the **hull** and engines, the accommodation, or both. Commonly, no breakdown between attention to these two general areas is made unless the refit is a major one. One must take with some degree of caution announcements of multi-million-dollar refits since, frequently, these amount to little more than routine maintenance of the ship including such hotel items as replacement of soft furnishings with others of similar design.

Refurbish
See **Refit**.

Registry
See **Country of Registry** and **Port of Registry**.

Repeat Cruisers
Anyone who has sailed at least once before and who is now sailing again with the same company.

Repositioning
See **Positioning Cruises**.

Repositioning Cruise
See **Positioning Cruises**.

Reservations Administration
Department including those taking reservations via telephone and which implements the recommendations of decision-making managers in **yield management** in terms of the prices to be charged for a given **cabin** or category of accommodation.

Reserve Buoyancy
Buoyancy possessed by a vessel that is in excess of what is needed to keep it afloat.

Retention Forcasting
The art and science of predicting how many passengers currently booked will cancel for any given sailing.

Revenue Accounting
Accounting subdepartment that handles revenue from cruise ticket, and cruise package sales.

Revenue Per Bed (RPD)
Phrase used at times to describe revenue per person per day.

Reverse Osmosis (R.O.)
Process of purifying salt water through desalination without evaporation as distillation.

Riding Crews
Cruise line or subcontractor repair crews that undertake repairs or refurbishment aboard a **cruise ship** while the vessel is in normal service.

Risk Management, Department of
Cruise line department concerned with most insurance matters. **Protection and Indemnity (P & I)** claims are, however, usually handled by the Loss Prevention Department.

River Cruises
River cruises have existed for perhaps a hundred years but became newly popular in the 1980's and 1990's. Of course, Rhine Cruises and those in some other European areas never lost their popularity. Some other well-known river **cruise areas** are the Mississippi, the Nile, the Danube, Yangtze as well

as those on French waterways. All the vessels engaged in this trade are purpose-built vessels with capacities ranging from ten to about three hundred passengers, except for those aboard some Delta Queen vessels which can be larger. River cruises are usually characterized by itineraries geared to the history, culture and heritage of the villages, towns and cities along the waterway. Barge cruising along canals in France and England have also become popular.

RMS

Abbreviation for "Royal Mail Ship," or a ship certified to carry the mail of Great Britain. This was commonly applied to line voyage ships and was invariably used when referring the Cunard *Queen Mary, Queen Elizabeth, Mauretania,* and other vessels.

Ro-ro Passenger Ship

A passenger ship with space for passenger vehicles that are loaded and unloaded in a roll-on, roll-off mode. Most **ferries** fall into this category. Many new ro-ro vessels have passenger accommodation that rivals that available aboard **cruise ships.** See also **Ferry**.

Roads

See **Roadstead**.

Roadstead (Roads)

Safe anchorage outside a harbor and well clear of shore. One of the most spectacular of these is off Singapore.

Roaring Forties

Region of the Southern Hemisphere between forty and fifty degrees South Latitude, this area extends around the globe with only limited interference from land. This area of the ocean is characterized by strong westerly winds and rough seas. **Cruise ships** regularly traverse parts of this region inasmuch as it includes the South Island of New Zealand, the seas south of Australia, the Tasman Sea (between Australia and New Zealand), and southern coastal waters of Chile and Argentina. The Cape of Good Hope, with its "Cape rollers," though north of the "Roaring Forties" is subject to

Roll

some of the same meteorological influences and has a wicked weather reputation.

Roll

The movement of a ship downward on the **port** or **starboard** side, creating a rolling motion. This is to a large extent corrected by **stabilizers**. This is in contrast to a **pitch**, which involves the vertical motion of the **bow**, and which cannot be corrected.

Rudder

A metal plate mounted vertically at the **stern** of a vessel that, when turned, changes the course of a ship. It is partly or completely underwater. Rudders are of several types according to the way they are designed and mounted. Often, there are two.

Running Down Clause

See **Hull & Machinery.**

S

S G & A

See **Selling General and Administration.**

Safety and Security Plan

Includes plans for fire safety, lifesaving, and damage control.

Safety Language

IMO provides that all ships must have a designated safety language, one that all crew are able to speak and in which all safety manuals are written.

Safety Management Manual

Provided for in the **International Safety Management Code (ISM)** which calls for the development of a **Safety Management System (SMS)** in all cruise lines. A copy of the manual outlining safety policies and procedures for staff both at sea and ashore is to be kept aboard the vessel at all times. The manual is also to include corporate organizational charts and contact lists for emergencies. See also **Safety Management System (SMS).**

Safety Management System (SMS)

The SMS is an important part of the **International Safety Management Code (ISM)** adopted by the **IMO.** (Part of chapter IX to the **SOLAS** convention in May 1994 that became effective on July 1, 1998). The SMS requires that every company develop, implement, and maintain a system that includes (1) a safety and environmental protection policy, (2) procedures to ensure safe operation of ships in compliance with all relevant laws, (3) defined levels of authority and lines of communication between departments at sea and on shore, (4) procedures for accident and violations of code, (5) procedures for responding to emergency situations, and (6) procedures for internal audit and management review. All this must be compiled in an accessible **safety management manual** and carried aboard a ship at all times.

Safety Of Life At Sea (SOLAS), International Convention for

With the full name of International Convention for the Safety of Life at Sea, the first convention was adopted by thirteen nations in 1914 following the sinking of the *Titanic*. Since then, there have been a number of other conventions, protocols, and amendments. These have had far-reaching influence on the design and operation of ships including rules for water-tight subdivision, materials that may be used, fire prevention, the design of life-saving appliances and the number that must be carried, and on many other aspects of marine architecture and operation. The 1997 amendments require substantial changes aboard many vessels. These include the following, among others: (1) Installation of automatic sprinkler and smoke detection systems in accommodation and service areas; (2) Placement of "low-location" emergency lighting along escape routes, similar to the lights lining the aisles of passenger planes; (3) Replacement of combustible materials, such as wood, with noncombustibles; (4) and the enclosing of key stairways. SOLAS regulations are a major factor in the planning and design of **cruise ships**. Compliance is monitored by each signatory country. The U.S. Coast Guard annually inspects every **cruise ship** taking on passengers at U.S. **ports**, serving as a guarantee that these ships meet all SOLAS requirements.

Sag

Refers to the situation where the frame of a ship is distorted, usually by stress, such that the center of the vessel is lower than **bow** and **stern**. This condition can be created by wave conditions or uneven distribution of weight, the latter mainly of concern to cargo operators. Sag is the opposite of **hog**, where bow and/or stern droop.

Sail Area

In the cruise industry, refers to the high wall-like sides of today's **cruise ships** which can catch the wind under severe conditions and, together with shallow draft, make them difficult to maneuver. Multiple thrusters mitigate to some extent, but do not eliminate, the factor of sail area in maneuvering a modern **cruise ship**. Also refers to the amount of sail a sailing ship can carry.

Sail Assisted

Sailing **cruise ship** where the primary means of propulsion is diesel. Sails are functional but supplementary.

Sailing Alongside

Used when describing two or more vessels sailing on the same or a similar itinerary.

Sailing Coordinator

Individual given responsibility for monitoring specified sales aspects of an individual itinerary. Responsibility may be general, or limited to **air/sea, yield management**, etc.

Sales Plateau

Volume of sales a travel agency needs to reach in order to qualify for an **override** (higher than standard) commission.

Salvage

Recovery of a wrecked vessel – one that has gone aground, sunk, or is badly damaged and helpless.

Sapo

A crew member who complains to another officer

about his own supervisor. This is a crew member's derogatory/slang word.

Saveall
(1) A small oblong pan at the base of the **porthole** to accommodate drips and prevent water from damaging cabinetry, used where **portholes** are kept open – a rarity in modern **cruise ships**; (2) a low wall built around equipment or fittings that may leak oil or water to contain anticipated leakages, e.g. around washing machines in a laundry.

Scantlings
Traditional marine term embracing measurement of components comprising a ship's **hull**. Taken together, they are a measure of hull strength. Thickness in hull plates is one aspect of this. Passengers embarking on the *Norway*, built as the Atlantic liner *France* for high-speed North Atlantic operation the year 'round, get a good illustration of the meaning of this term in the thickness of hull plates through which they must pass to board the ship.

Schooner
A sail-powered or sail-assisted vessel with more than one **mast** with sails aligned in a **fore**-and-**aft** direction. The foremast is lower than the after mast(s). This is in contrast with a **square-rigger** where the sails are carried on yards that are at right angles to the **keel**.

Scrap, Sold for
Eventual fate of almost every **cruise ship** that does not become a marine casualty. Sale is by **light-weight tonnage** and includes all furnishings unless other arrangements are made. Many fixtures gain new life in the homes and businesses in the ship-breaking country. In the 1990's, most ships have been scrapped in India and Pakistan.

Screw
A ship's **propeller**. Most **cruise ships** are twin-screw vessels, i.e. have two propellers.

Scupper
Drains in the **hull** of a ship at **deck** level to allow water that has come on board, or that has accumulated from cleaning, to flow back into the sea.

Scuttle
 (1) **Porthole**; also referred to as a **sidescuttle**; (2) intentionally to sink one's own ship.

Sea Chest
 Opening in the bottom of a ship that allows the intake of ocean water for such functions as engine cooling, air conditioning, desalination, and for other purposes.

Sea Saver Fares
 One of the first discount cruise plans, introduced in the early eighties by Norwegian Caribbean Line (now Norwegian Cruise Line or NCL). Subsequently, other firms started to offer a variety of discount schemes. In the early eighties, roughly coinciding with the entry into service of NCL's *Norway* (formerly French Line's *France*), the capacity of the cruise industry began to expand and discounting was introduced to help fill the increased number of **berths**. Actually, Sea Savers were a form of stand-by where the consumer chose the sailing date and the line chose the ship and itinerary.

Sea Trials
 Final, comprehensive set of trials prior to delivery of a vessel to owners. A *Code for Sea Trials* (1973) is published by the Society of Naval Architects and Marine Engineers in its Technical & Research Code C2. This outlines and describes an extensive list of tests to be included which amount to a comprehensive testing of a ship's systems under stated conditions. This is available for adoption by a cruise line in prescribing sea trial procedures, and satisfactory completion of them, prior to acceptance of a vessel.

Seafarer
 Traditional term for crew member.

Seafarer's Agreement (Contract)
 A crew member's employment contract.

Seafarer's Manual
 Manual describing crew rules and regulations for conduct on board.

Seafarers' Hours of Work and Manning of Ships Convention, 1996

See **International Labor Organization (ILO) Maritime Conference**.

Seaman's Book

Book containing information about the individual **crew** member including training that has received, dates of service on board current and previous ships, and other information. This is required by some flag **administrations**.

Seaman's Will

Sign-off status indicating separation from the ship was voluntary.

Seating Request, Special

Often, agents will request for their clients not only a specific dining room, table size, or seating, a specific dining room area or table number(s). Special seating requests are especially common for groups.

Seatrade

An organization concerned with communication among those in the cruise industry or doing business with it. The *Seatrade Cruise Industry Convention* covers all facets of the industry and is held in Miami during March of each year. The meeting, an annual event since 1985, is supplemented by other regional Seatrade cruise conventions in Europe, Asia, and Australia. The British-based Seatrade Organisation publishes a magazine for the cruise industry, *Seatrade Cruise Review*, and operates a management training company, the *Seatrade Cruise Academy*.

Seaway

In the cruise industry, most often refers to a sea condition of high waves and the behavior of a given ship under these circumstances. For example, "She is a comfortable ship in a seaway." Outside of the industry, the term most often refers to a waterway, channel, or canal.

Seaworthy

Where the condition of a ship permits it to sail in safety on the ocean. The term is usually used following repair of damage, or to express a ship's ability to move under its own power, in spite of being damaged, in safety. While this must be one of the most frequently used generic maritime terms, it is also used in legal documents to reflect the obligation of an owner, charterer, or other operator to maintain a ship in safe and appropriate condition for service.

Secondary Reservation Center

Reservation center away from the principal one which can be undertaken for a number of reasons. In 1997, Royal Caribbean International and Carnival Cruise Lines became the first cruise lines to open additional reservation centers in locations away from corporate headquarters in Miami. In both cases, the move was undertaken because the operations had outgrown the labor pool available in Miami and because there was a perceived need to have an alternative office available in the event of a major direct hurricane strike on Miami.

Security, Shore-Side

Provided either by the **port** or, under contract, by the cruise line. Assures passenger safety during **embarkation** and **disembarkation**; controls access to the vessel; provides luggage security; staffs metal detectors screening embarking passengers; and other duties. Those maintaining security aboard ship are unable to be used ashore, either because they are required on board at all times or because local labor laws do not allow their deployment ashore.

Segment Cruises

See **Cruise Segments**.

Seizure

See **Arrest**.

Selling General and Administration (SG&A)

Expenses incurred by a cruise line other than those involved in operating a ship. Some items are on the borderline of this category, e.g. embarkation staff.

Separation Zone

Area between two designated shipping lanes established in areas of heavy commercial traffic. See also **Traffic Separation Scheme**.

Service Spaces

Defined by **SOLAS** to include galleys, pantries with

cooking equipment, lockers, mail and specie rooms, store rooms, workshops outside of machinery spaces, similar spaces and trunks to them. This definition reflects general usage.

Seven-day Equivalent

A measure used to standardize productivity comparison of source markets. For example, in comparing the number of passengers a company attracts from France and Germany, this measure evens the number of **passenger cruise days (PCD's)** that go with each unit of headcount.

Shaft Tunnel

Elongated compartment surrounding the propeller shaft that makes it possible to inspect and service the shaft, glands, and bearings. New podded propulsion units make all this unnecessary.

Share Basis

Sales definition of a **cabin** shared by two unrelated passengers not travelling together.

Shared Cabin

See **Share Basis**.

Sheer

In most vessels of the ocean **liner** era, **bow** and **stern** were higher than the midships section, introducing a graceful curve to the vessel's lines and decks. The traditional purpose was to keep top decks at **bow** and **stern** as dry as possible. For the most part, sheer is now found only in classic **cruise ships.**

Shell Door

A door through the side of a ship's **hull**, or **shell plating**. Such openings are often used to **embark** and **disembark** passengers, and are generally required to load and unload stores, luggage on major ships, and machinery.

Shell Plating

External steel **hull** plating.

Ship Arrest

See **Arrest**.

Ship Broker

A person or a company specializing in selling ships. Usually, ship brokers are involved in chartering, buying, and selling ships. They negotiate the terms and conditions of sale or charter and are usually compensated by commission, a fee sometimes shared by parties in a transaction.

Ship Buffs

Ship enthusiasts which, according to Cruise Lines International Association, represent 10% of the cruise market or more.

Ship Chandler

An individual or company selling, and often delivering, equipment and supplies for ships.

Ship Identification Number (IMO Number)

Such a number, conforming to the **IMO** ship identification number scheme, is required of all passenger ships of one hundred or more gross tons.

Ship Manager

An agent or manager appointed by the shipowner to provide operational shore support for a ship. The ship manager tracks condition, maintenance, repairs needed, and may supervise the turnaround. Sometimes known as a husband, the function is more that of a servant or shore coordinator, ensuring that shore-based deck and engine services and hotel support are available when needed. In some lines, responsibilities in relation to the ship are more sweeping, extending to such areas as performance and profitability.

Ship Operating Expenses

Operating costs associated with a vessel, as opposed to those incurred by the shore establishment. Some are clearly ship expenses: food and beverage, fuel, port taxes, etc. Others are in a gray area and subject to arbitrary determination or, in the case of charters, negotiation: embarkation costs, information systems support, communications with the ship, and other items.

Ship Profile

(1) A vessel's outline when viewed from abreast; (2) ship's outline represented in a broadside cutaway plan illustrating the interior and outline;

Short International Voyage (SIV)

(3) brief narrative description with summary information concerning a ship.

Ship Under Contract
Where a ship has been ordered but actual construction has not yet begun. Once actual fabrication has begun, the term "under construction" is appropriate.

Ship's Agent
See **Port Agent**.

Ship's Paper (Ship's Documents)
A set of documents that needs to be kept on board the vessel at all times and is required by various local, state, federal and international authorities when entering and leaving **ports**. These documents include, among others, the ship's registry, charter party, agreement, the vessel's local coast guard certificate, public health certificate, and other similar documents.

Ship's Registry (Country of Registry)
Term commonly used for flag **administration**.

Ship's Will
Crew sign-off status; indicates that separation was involuntary.

Shore Excursions
Organized trips ashore at ports of call, most often operated by an independent contractor, for passengers in groups of varying sizes. These almost always feature the services of a guide. Shore excursions may be for sightseeing, entertainment, and are also occasionally combined with transfers.

Shore Tour
See **Shore Excursion**.

Shorex
See **Shore Excursion**.

Short International Voyage (SIV)
A cruise in which the ship is never more than two hundred miles from **port**, or another place where passengers can be **disembarked** in safety; also, to quote **SOLAS**, "Neither the distance between the last port of call in the country in which the voyage begins and the final port of destination nor the return voyage shall exceed 600 miles." This is important because of its impact on the number of life-

saving appliances that must be on board. When the former Royal Cruise Line ship *Golden Odyssey* was sold to Star Cruises for operation in coastal waters, capacity could be increased in a major way without an increase in the number of lifeboats. Distances are related to the range of rescue helicopters.

Shoulder Season

The period immediately before or right after the main season. Actual months vary from area to area. In Alaska, for instance, the Shoulder Season consists of May and part of June, as well as September.

Show Galley

A galley that is an integral part of a dining room (usually a buffet restaurant) that serves both to prepare and display the food about to be served.

Sidescuttle

Porthole. Also referred to as **scuttle**.

Sight Lines

Clear sight lines are important in designing theater-style showrooms that serve as venues for production shows. One of the great modern challenges of interior design is to provide entertainment venues with a minimum number of seats with obstructed views. This is also a factor in the view from the **bridge**. Even though most passenger ships no longer carry cargo or containers on **deck**, and the number of **masts** has been reduced, this can still be a problem. In the 1940's through the 1960's, the British built a fleet of passenger ships for Orient, P & O, and Union Castle where the bridge was **amidships** and offered close to a 360 degree view. This feature can still be seen on Premier's *IslandBreeze* and *OceanBreeze*. Normally, bridge views aft are available only from the **bridge wings**. Wings also allow a view of the **waterline** when coming **alongside**.

Sign Off

When a seaman's contract ends and the individual leaves the vessel. At this point, he is deleted from the crew list.

Sign On

When a crew member joins a vessel and is added to the crew list.

Singing

Noise made when a **propeller** resonates at certain frequencies that can be heard throughout the **stern** area of the ship. This occurs under one or more of the following circumstances: the propeller has not been installed properly; design is not optimal; or, the propeller has been damaged in some way.

Single Compartment Standard

Standard applying to vessels able to remain afloat if not more than one compartment is flooded; this does not comply with **SOLAS** standards and has not for many years. However, local authorities may permit operation in coastal waters of ships with this standard simply by not enforcing the SOLAS regulation.

Singles Program

Where passengers may book **berths** in a **cabin** independently. Strangers sharing cabins must, of course, be of the same sex and, generally, be over the age of eighteen. Policies differ from line to line.

Sister Ship to…

Built to the same design as…. Currently, most ships are built in pairs or series because of the substantial economies obtainable in building additional ships to the same design. Construction costs are lower, design expenses far less, and a cruise line can still improve slightly on the original design without eliminating most economies that are available. However, lines still seek to give to each ship a unique personality derived through differences in color schemes and decoration so that passengers feel they are getting a different, if equivalent, cruise experience when they sail on Sister ships of the same company.

Sittings, Late and Early

Most **cruise ships** have two sittings for dinner, and sometimes for breakfast and lunch as well. The first dinner sitting is generally at 6:15 or 6:30, and the second, about two hours later. A number of five-star ships do offer one-sitting dining, but command fares that justify the very considerable cost of providing this amenity.

Skipper

Slang term for **captain** or **master**. Another: "Old Man."

Slamming

When waves pound a ship's **bow**, or when there is severe **pitching**, most commonly in a **head sea**. This causes a shuddering motion and a loud report. Slamming can do damage, especially to a modern **cruise ship** with lighter **scantlings** than the Atlantic **liners** designed for rough seas, and is sometimes a signal to the **captain** to order reduced speed or slight change of course. Naval architects define a slam when two criteria have been met: (1) bow emergence, and (2) exceeding a threshold velocity.

Slot Tech

A critical member of casino staff whose job is to repair slot machines. Since the process of opening the machines provides access to the cash within, the position is considered to be a responsible one in the casino hierarchy.

Sludge Removal

Over a period of time, sludge from storage of liquids accumulates and cannot be discharged into the ocean. This is removed by truck in ports for recycling or disposal.

Smokestack

See **Funnel**.

SMS

See **Safety Management System**.

Sneeze Guard

Plastic or glass panels on buffets where food is displayed and passengers help themselves. These minimize the possibility that germs exhaled by passengers will reach the food.

Sneeze Shield

See **Sneeze Guard**.

Soft Furnishings

Carpeting, upholstery, bedspreads and other similar furnishings that are part of decor.

Software

Cuisine, service and entertainment aboard ship - as opposed to the vessel's physical attributes.

SOLAS
See **Safety of Life at Sea (SOLAS), International Convention for.**

Source Market
Passengers point of origin, usually expressed in geographic terms. The term can be applied to any number of passengers, from those in an entire fleet to a single group organized by a travel agent.

Southern Caribbean, Cruises To
A leading cruise area south and east of San Juan extending to the North Coast of South America. To be reached on a seven-day itinerary, such cruises must originate in ports such as San Juan, Barbados, Aruba, or the Dominican Republic. Along with cruises from South Florida to the Eastern and Western Caribbean, Southern Caribbean cruises now command some of the cruise lines' largest and finest ships.

Space Ratio
See **Passenger Space Ratio.**

Special Entertainment Cruises
Sailings where the advertised feature is a star entertainer or other special entertainment.

Special Interest Cruises
Cruises where special activity or entertainment features are calculated to attract those with a special interest e.g. sports, bridge, music, etc.

Spindrift
When, due to high wind and gale conditions, wave tops are blown into spray.

Spoilage
(1) **Cabins** vacant on sailing day; (2) unused cabins from a group block that are not used by the agency reserving the block of cabins. The latter cabins may, in fact, have been rebooked by sailing day.

Sponsons
Projections from the side of a vessel, installed for one of several reasons. Some ships have had these installed at the **waterline** in order to meet the requirements of **SOLAS** for adequate stability when top weight has been added to a ship during rebuilding or **refit**. In other instances, these have been installed at **deck** level to increase **lido deck** area. Traditionally, the word has been used most

often in a naval context when sponsons have been installed to permit the mounting of additional armament, most often anti aircraft guns.

Sponsor

Traditional name for one who christens or names a ship at time of launching. Currently, the naming ceremony is a major media event, occurs following a ship's completion, and the sponsor is referred to as a ship's **godmother**.

Square Rigger

Sail-powered or **sail-assisted** vessel where sails are square-rigged and aligned at right angles to the **keel**.

Squat

(1) Where the **trim** of a ship is affected by hydrodynamic forces such that the **stern** of the ship settles lower in the water; (2) where the stern of a ship gives the impression of **hoging** or drooping that may reflect reality or merely the ship's absence of **sheer** combined with **hull** lines. The first condition is especially likely to occur when a ship is sailing in shallow water.

SS

See **Steam Ship** and **Turbine Steam Ship**.

Stability

The ability of a vessel to remain upright in any condition, damaged or otherwise. This is measured in terms of metacentric height. This is the distance between the calculated ship's virtual center of roll (metacenter) and the ship's center of gravity. If the center of gravity is below the metacenter, the metacentric height is positive and the ship is said to be stable i.e. will tend to return to an upright orientation when heeled over. If the center of gravity is above the metacenter, the ship has negative stability and the ship will tend to roll to one side (loll), and in an extreme case will capsize. Aside from safety, there are practical ramifications for the **cruise ship** passenger. A ship with a great metacentric height will be what is known as a "stiff, snappy roller" – too stable, the ship snaps back from a roll so quickly that the effect is uncomfortable. A comparatively low metacentric height makes for a slow, easy roll comfortable in swells. Obviously, what is needed is a compromise between the demands of safety and comfort. Shipowners and designers must be careful of the impact of a refit – new facilities, added weight high in the ship, on a vessel's metacentric height.

Stability Book

The stability of a vessel changes from cruise to cruise as the result of such variables as fuel, water, stores carried and consumed, number of passengers and cargo (if any), as well as other factors. For each deployment or itinerary, a stability book is prepared taking into consideration the specific consumption profile of that itinerary or deployment. This guides officers in adjusting fuel and other ballast so that the ship will be kept on an even keel and remain in safe operation.

Stabilized Antenna

Antenna built so that it maintains its focus on the appropriate satellite regardless of the ship's course changes. In order to do so, it rotates horizontally and vertically.

Stabilizer

Moving fin(s) on both sides of a **cruise ship** that, through changing their attitude or angle, counteract a vessel's roll. The first major passenger ship so fitted was the P & O liner *Chusan* of 1950.

Stacks

See **Funnel**.

Staff Captain

The second in command; is a licensed **Captain** as well as the Captain's deputy (represents the Captain when the Captain is not on board the vessel). He is responsible for all maintenance, radio communications, security, medical services and the discipline aboard the vessel. The responsibilities of Staff Captains vary from one cruise line to another. The Staff Captain position does not exist on cargo vessel, but is very important on **cruise ships.** Sometimes referred to as Chief Officer.

Stairwell Enclosure

One of the many demanding provisions of the 1997 Amendments to **SOLAS** is that stairwells be separated from surrounding areas. This seeks to isolate a major avenue for the spread of fires aboard ship. Such ships as *Norway* and *Rembrandt, ex-Rotterdam*, have had this work undertaken.

Stand By

For a ship responding to a distress signal, to wait for further orders relative to rescue or salvage; to wait for further orders generally.

Stand On

To maintain present course.

Standards of Training Certification and Watchkeeping for Seafarers (STCW)

This IMO convention came into force in 1984. It established, for the first time, internationally accepted minimum standards for crew. It is not necessarily the basis for crew requirements in all states; many have higher standards. The convention was revised in 1995 and standards increased. STCW certificates are now required by many nations for ships' officers.

Starboard

The right side of a ship as viewed when facing forward.

Stateroom

In connotation, a stateroom is a large, well-equipped cabin, not necessarily a cabin deluxe. In normal usage, the terms "cabin" and "stateroom" are often used interchangeably.

STCW

See **Standards or Training Certification and Watchkeeping for Seafarers.**

Steamship

A ship powered by steam, almost always in the few steamships still in service by means of steam turbines. In the past, other types of steam propulsion have been used. On board the pre-war French liner *Normandie* and a number of other contemporary ships, the means of propulsion was steam-generated electricity and electric motor. This had the advantage of great flexibility in efficient speed when a ship cruised, and the disadvantages of greater initial cost and dispersion of some of the energy generated in transmission to the motor. *Titanic* was powered by a combination of reciprocating steam engines and a low-pressure turbine to use left-over steam from the major machinery. Most steamships built have used turbines with gearing for the transition necessary between the high revolutions of the turbines and the low revolutions of the propellers. A steamship generally bears the prefix "SS" as compared with a diesel ship's "MV" (**motor vessel**) or "MS" (Motor Ship). There have been other variations, such as TSS (**Turbine Steamship**). None of these are to be confused with "**RMS**" which, for British vessels, means "Royal Mail Ship," one with a license to carry Britain's mail.

Steering Gear Control System
Provides for control of the ship by allowing transmission of orders from the **bridge** to steering mechanism.

Stern
The rear portion of a vessel. Normally, this refers to the **aft**-most section of the **hull**, though in the modern **cruise ship**, the hull may be indistinguishable from the superstructure at the **stern**.

Stern Platform
Open area at the **stern** of a ship, usually removed from passenger **decks**, containing **bollards** and ropes used in mooring the vessel. In the new superships, this is generally several deck levels down from open passenger decks at the stern – low enough for convenient work with mooring bollards and **lineman** on shore.

Stern Thrusters
See **Bow Thrusters**.

Stevedoring
Stevedoring is the service that is used by ships to load and unload passenger luggage as well as stores in **ports**. Those performing this service are called stevedores.

Stores
Normally refers to all the supplies needed to main-

tain a ship at sea – food, supplies needed to maintain equipment, etc. The term is usually not applied to fuel or spare parts.

Stowaways

Those travelling aboard ship illegally without a ticket or other authorization for passage. This is a major problem inasmuch as cruise lines incur stiff fines for transporting illegal emigrants. In an age when terrorism is an ongoing concern, stowaways also constitute a potential security problem. This is a far cry from the days when stowaways were thought of as those following a romantic notion of travelling free and seeing the world.

Stretching (Lengthening, Jumboising)

Involves cutting a **cruise ship** in two and inserting a newly-built section. Ships have been stretched for decades, beginning in the period following World War I. What generally results is a major increase in capacity achieved in a shorter time than building a completely new ship and with almost no sacrifice in speed. The first modern **cruise ship** to be stretched was Royal Caribbean's *Song of Norway* in 1978. Tonnage increased from 18,416 to 23,005, length from 550 to 637 feet, and passenger capacity from 876 to 1196. *Nordic Prince* was given a similar enlargement following success of the *Song*. Most ambitious stretching to date was of Holland America's *Westerdam* in 1989/90. The ex-*Homeric* went from 42,092 gross tons and 669 feet in length to 53,872 tons and a length of 800 feet.

Structural Cross Section

Cross section of a ship illustrating just the structural components of the vessel – the decks, double bottom, supporting columns, and over-all shape. May be either a longitudinal (laid out in a **fore** and **aft** direction) or a transverse cross section (laid out across the ship).

Subdivision Load Line

According to **SOLAS**, the "...**waterline** used in determining the subdivision of the ship." The same source defines *deepest subdivision load line* as "...the waterline which corresponds to the greatest draught permitted by the subdivision requirements which are applicable."

Superliner

Suez Canal Tonnage Certificate

Tonnage figure on the basis of which Suez Canal tolls are assessed. Different from standard tonnage figures and assigned by flag **administration** or **classification society**.

Suite

Deluxe accommodation aboard ship, sometimes consisting of separate bed and sitting rooms. Often, however, the term is applied to cabins deluxe with separate bed and sitting areas rather than rooms.

Sun Deck

Generic name for an open **deck** area for passengers that is one of the highest decks aboard. While this may be the deck with pool, lido, and bars, the specificity of meaning for this term has been lost over the years.

Superfast Ferry

A new breed of **ferry**, without overnight accommodation, capable of speeds of forty **knots** and more. These are smaller than traditional ferries, count their passage time in terms of a few hours rather than overnight, and can be extremely useful as **cruise ship** tenders or as shore excursion vessels. They can be of catamaran, monohull, hydrofoil, or other innovative design.

Superliner

Term normally applied to ocean liners exceeding approximately 40,000 gross register tons in size. This is not an exact designation, and some would apply them only to liners exceeding 50,000 tons. This term arose from the relative size of ships built in the 1920's and 1930's, but probably came into standard usage with the advent of the Cunard Queens, *United States*, and *France*, mostly in the post-World War II period. When **cruise ships** began to grow notably in size, beginning with the advent of Carnival's *Holiday* of 46,052 GRT in 1985, and was immediately followed by two near-sisters of equal size, the term was applied to *Holiday*, *Jubilee*, and *Celebration*. Since most new **cruise ships** fall into this size category at the present time, and there is growing appreciation of the difference between the design of a modern

cruise ship and an ocean liner, the term has fallen into disuse.

Superstructure

That part of a ship's structure above the **hull**. On sailing ships, these consisted merely of **deck houses**. With the advent of the steamship, deck houses grew larger to accommodate public rooms and, eventually, **cabins**. In many ways, the development of the steamship as a comfortable and even luxurious means of travel can be measured by the increase in size of the superstructure.

Survey

An evaluation of a ship's condition, design, and structural attributes to determine the extent to which the ship qualifies for its intended **class**. See also **in class**.

Surveyor

One who conducts, on behalf of a **classification society**, a survey to determine whether a vessel is "**in Class**" – that is, meets the design and condition requirements to operate safely within its Class. See also **class, in class,** and **classification society**.

Survival Craft Equipment

SOLAS prescribes the supplies and equipment that must be present in each type of survival craft to sustain survivors until rescue – life boats, rafts, etc. These include such items as buoyant oars, buckets, survival manual, **binnacle** containing a compass, anchor, water receptacle or de-salting apparatus, whistle, anti-seasickness medicine, jack-knife, manual water pump, fishing tackle, tool box, fire extinguishing equipment, flares, smoke signals, and other items.

T

Tail Shaft

Aft end of a ship's **propeller** shaft.

Take

See **Net Win**.

TBA

"To be assigned." At times it is necessary to issue a ticket before a cabin is assigned. At such times, passengers are advised of specific cabin assignment on check-in.

Teak Decks

Teak, a native timber from Southeast Asia, is the material of choice for **cruise ship decks**. It is durable, attractive, easily maintained, and pleasant under foot. No really satisfactory substitute has been found. Carpeting attracts moisture, fades, and is never replaced often enough. Disadvantages of teak include high initial cost and weight. Even **cruise ships** that provide teak decks through much of the ship often revert to other materials for their highest decks. Notable exceptions: the new ships of Carnival and Holland America. By and large, the industry has settled on this material as making the most sense in the design of new ships because of its attractiveness to passengers and its fine durability. However, a major source of this wood – Burma (Myamar) is restricting production to increase the price.

Technical Water

See **Non-potable Fresh Water**.

Telegraph, Bridge/Engine Room

Instrument used on older ships to communicate engine speed and direction from the **bridge** to the **engine room**. The telegraph was usually of polished brass, with white dial and black markings. Now, engines are controlled directly from the bridge without personal intervention in the engine room.

Tender

A small boat that carries passengers between a **cruise ship** and shore when the vessel is unable to **dock** and must anchor offshore. Tenders may double as life boats and be included in the lifeboat complement of the vessel. Shore-based tenders are also used at times. Presently, non-Greek ships are prevented from using their own tenders while in

Greek ports unless the local operator cannot perform this service (in which case he still receives a fee). Tendering is becoming less common as harbor facilities improve.

Terminal Port

Port where a ship is based and begins and ends most cruises. A ship may have several terminal ports at different times of the year, usually one for each deployment. In modern cruise-line usage, it is often referred to as "home base." See also **Home Port**.

Territorial Waters

Waters generally within three miles or one marine league of a particular landmass. The territorial waters of a particular country are sometimes extended by law to protect a country's environment or economic interests.

Theme Cruises

A cruise where some or all on board activities are intended to attract people with a special interest in the theme area. This has been used by many companies to fill ships during fringe seasons. NCL has been very successful with its sports theme cruises. One of the more exotic theme efforts: the music and drama cruises of Paquet's *Mermoz*. For the music cruises ("Le Festivale Musique en Mer"), the cruise staff are sent on leave and their place taken by musicians and those managing events centered on classical music. However, themes can also involve only a subset of passengers and can either totally dominate a sailing or be designed to appeal to only a small group of those on board.

Theoretical Revenue

Cruise ship or cruise line revenue based on brochure prices. Given the prevalence of discounting in today's cruise industry, this is very theoretical indeed. However, it is a useful concept in measuring the actual level of discounting and to judge the effectiveness of **yield management** systems as well as market conditions.

Ticketed Shows

A concept, used aboard NCL's *Norway* and now by Disney, where passengers are given tickets in an effort to control the volume of passengers attending any given show. This is useful where the size of the showroom cannot accommodate half the passenger list (and be able to admit passengers from both early and late dining room sittings on the same evening); where superstar entertainment is likely to draw many repeat viewers; or where different shows are offered to passengers on the same evening and any individual venue is unable to accommodate all the passengers who might attend at any one time.

Tiered Commission Structure

A graduated scale of commissions paid to travel agents for cruise sales based on volume or other measure set forth in a contractual agreement between seller and cruise line. Commissions higher than the lowest level (commonly 10%) are also referred to as **overrides**.

Time Charter

An agreement where the owner charters the vessel to an operator, but the owner continues to provide **deck** and engine services and perhaps others, depending on the agreed-upon terms. The duration of the charter may be defined by time or by number of voyages on a given route.

Tipping Policies

Cruise lines have a variety of policies that relate to tipping. Most lines share with passengers tipping guidelines that indicate the level of gratuities expected by staff and management. However, there are several other policies used by the industry today: (1) *No tipping*, a policy used by Seabourn where gratuities are refused if offered. (2) *No tipping required*, typified by Holland America Cruises. This policy does not prohibit tipping but indicates, as the phrase suggests, that it is not required. (3) *Pooled tipping*, such as is practiced by Greek companies, where gratuities are presented centrally and redistributed by shipboard management to all staff who qualify for them. (4) *Prepaid tipping*, used by a number of North America-based cruise lines for passengers from Europe and other areas where tipping on the customary scale is not in the culture. This strategy is also sometimes used for groups where there may be the impression that tips are included in the basic fare. The money, once collected, is redistributed directly to staff serving the passengers.

Tivoli Lights

Chain of lights strung between the **bow, mast, funnel**, and **stern** (some or all of the preceding), illuminated while in **port**.

Total Loss

(1) **Constructive total loss**: the cost to remove and repair the wreck is higher than the insured value; (2) Compromised/agreed loss: the cost of removal and repair is very close to the insured value. Both sides agree to a total monetary figure to be paid in compensation for the loss.

Tradewinds

Winds that blow with great regularity from west to east in the region within thirty degrees both north and south of the Equator. They have some impact on cruise operations generally and, in the case of the northeast trades, those in the Caribbean. **Cruise ships** sailing from South Florida to the Virgin Islands generally sail into a ten to fifteen mile-per-hour headwind, causing breezy conditions on **deck** and fractionally slowing the ship. In the reverse direction, the winds tend to almost equal the speed of the ship, assisting the vessel's progress but causing stuffy conditions on deck.

Trading

An expression from the maritime industry referring to the fact that a vessel is operating / sailing, in contrast to the situation where a vessel is **laid up**.

Trading Limitations

When a **cruise ship** changes hands, and especially when sold by one of the major cruise operators, there will often be "non-compete" clauses in the sale agreement preventing the vessel from operating in competition with the seller's fleet. These limitations are often defined in the form of days that can be spent in any given market under the new ownership. Thus, when Carnival Corporation sold *Festivale* to Premier, there was a limit to the number of days that the ship could operate in the Caribbean market.

Traffic Separation Scheme (TSS)

Agreed-on traffic lanes for ships in straits and other waters where there is chronic heavy traffic. In the United States, the TSS was designed and implemented by the U.S. Coastguard in areas of heavy commercial traffic. It consists of two one-mile lanes separated by a two-mile-wide "Separation Zone."

Training Pay

A special payment given to **crew** members for participating in specified hotel training; provided for in several international maritime agreements.

Transcanal Cruise

The term is generally used to denote cruises that provide a complete transit of the Panama Canal in either direction. These cruises are popular features of North American cruise itineraries and provide a great deal of revenue both as cruise series and as **positioning cruises** between West Coast and Caribbean cruise areas. See also **Partial Transit**.

Transit Passengers

(1) Passengers who stay on board a vessel for a second cruise when a vessel completes a cruise itinerary. This situation arises when **back-to-back** cruises are purchased and makes desirable special arrangements for guests during the day prior to sailing. Options can include remaining on board (depending on local regulations), special shore excursions, or transportation to shopping centers or other attractions; (2) by literal definition, the status of cruise passengers at ports of call.

Trials

See **Berth Trials, Sea Trials, Yard Trials**.

Trim

Measures the degree to which **bow** and **stern** are on the same level i.e. have the same draft. A damaged ship where the down angle of the bow is five degrees is said to be down by the head by five degrees. Trimming tanks facilitate control of trim. Considerations regarding trim are one more reason for the proper control of weight during the construction process. When complete, P & O Line's *Canberra* was found to be down by the stern by five feet. Draconian measures were necessary to get the ship back into trim, including the addition of permanent **ballast** which increased the ship's **draft**, something that was a constraint in using the vessel for cruises.

Troop Ship

In the days before submarines became extremely fast and aircraft large, the main means of transporting troops to an area of conflict was by ship. In major wars, these were often former passenger and **cruise ships**. Cunard's *Queen Mary* and *Queen Elizabeth* have been credited, rightly or wrongly, in shortening World War II by one year because of the extensive trooplift they provided from North America to Europe. The extreme usefulness of passenger ships in both world wars gave rise to construction of a fleet of American passenger and **cruise ships** with heavy government subsidies and "defence features" so that they could easily be converted to troopships in time of war. Many of these are still in service. They include the *Independence* of American Hawaii Cruises, built for American Export Lines as an Atlantic Liner with a cruising speed of 22.5 **knots** and a potential cruising speed, in time of war, of 25 knots; and the *Enchanted Seas* and *Enchanted Isle* of Commodore Cruise Line, built as the *Brasil* and *Argentina* respectively for cruise and line service between New York and Buenos Aires. The arrangement also involved extensive operating subsidies paid by the U.S. Government. When submarines were constructed that could achieve 40 **knots** and more under water, the concept of placing thousands of troops on these ships in hostile waters became obsolete. Subsidies were withdrawn and most of the ships taken out of service and, after a period of layup, sold to non-U.S. operators. It is a testament to U.S. shipbuilders and designers of the day that most of these ships are still in cruise service. The only major exceptions: the *Santa Paula* built for Grace Line, shelled during the invasion of Kuwait; and the *Constitution*, built for American Export, which sank en route to the shipbreakers in 1997.

Trunk

Term used extensively in naval architecture to denote a vertical passageway provided for technical or operational purposes. It is used to describe such varied spaces as exhaust pipes from engine room to funnel, hatchways to a cargo hold, the base of a swimming pool, escape passages, ventilation ducts, and others. This is not to be confused with the traditional "steamer trunk," a large hinged box used by some transatlantic passengers early in this century to house clothes and other personal effects.

TSS

See **Turbine Steam Ship**.

Tumble-home

Design situation where a ship is broader at the waterline than at the top of the **hull**. This was a feature of many express passenger liners with highly refined hull lines. The shape at the waterline was hydrodynamically optimum, whereas the width higher in the hull reflected considerations of weight, the passenger accommodation, and the structural requirements of the vessel and its intended service. Hull tumble-home helped to give to many of the classic passenger ships a sculptural beauty lacking in modern cruise vessels.

Turbine Steam Ship

Turbines have been the most widely-used form of propulsion for steamships in the Twentieth Century. Instead of using cylinders, turbines employ **rotors** and blades with much greater efficiency and greater potential speed. The first large passenger turbine ships were Cunard's 32,000-ton *Lusitania* and *Mauretania* which, between them, immediately captured the transatlantic speed record from German liners that still employed reciprocating steam machinery. The designation Turbine Steam Ship is usually shortened to "SS" and, less often, "TSS". For most of the Twentieth Century, this was generally a more quiet and comfortable means of passenger ship propulsion than the diesel. The advantage ended, however, with the perfection of diesel electric machinery mounted on "rafts" within a ship's hull rather than bolted directly to it. First turbine passenger ship was Cunard's 19,524-ton *Carmania*, in 1905, prototype for the two 1907 record-breakers.

Turning Basin

An area within a harbor of sufficient size for ships to turn around. Adjoins the deep-water entrance to the **port**, but can be located either at the inner end of the channel (as in Miami) or in the outer **harbor** (Nassau).

Two for One Pricing

Perhaps the most organized form of **fire sale** pricing, this is a common strategy for increasing bookings on "soft" sailings. Since the full brochure price is usually the basis for this, loss to the cruise line is not as great as might be imagined and what results is not only a very marketable concept but a good discounted rate for the passenger. For cruise lines, the pain can also be lessened by not including airfare or taxes for the second passenger.

Two-Compartment Standard

A vessel can remain afloat if not more than two compartments are flooded. This is the current minimum standard for ocean-going **cruise ships**.

U

Unbroached Lubricant

Unopened, unused lubricants aboard ship still in the original container. When buying, selling, or chartering a vessel on a bare-boat basis, an inventory is made of consumables on board (i.e., water, fuel, food, lubricants). These commodities are therefore accounted for in the transaction. Lubricants that have been removed from their original containers or that are contained in the vessel's machinery are not counted in the consumable inventory.

Unbundled Pricing

Pricing that breaks out individual elements of a package, allowing the consumer to purchase or not purchase each individually. Perhaps the most significant element in unbundled pricing is air transportation. **Port** charges are now most commonly included in the basic price of the cruise fare even in an unbundled pricing situation.

Uncharted

A reference to an object that does not appear on any charter/nautical map. This can be a rock, a wreck, or other underwater phenomenon. Alaskan Coastal waters are notorious for uncharted rocks. In the Atlantic near Nantucket, one caused $30 million in damage to the *QE2*. Further afield, the Dutch liner *Klipfontein* struck uncharted rocks five miles off the coast of Southern Africa and sank in forty-five minutes. Fortunately, all passengers were rescued.

UNCLOS

See **United Nations Conventions on Law of the Sea.**

Under Contract (Vessel)

A ship that has been ordered by a cruise line from a shipyard. Construction may or may not have started. This is in contrast with "letter of intent" status.

Under Way

Denotes that a ship has sailed, or is sailing – and is not anchored, moored, or aground.

Unearned Passenger Revenue (Advance Ticket Sales Revenue)

Money that has been placed on deposit by future passengers in the course of making a reservation. Depending on the policy of the line, at some point during the reservation period this becomes payment in full. Lay term for this money is "customer deposits" or "advance ticket sales revenue." These funds are shown on a company's books as a liability rather than an asset, though they do earn interest for the cruise line. They become operating revenue on either the first or last day of a cruise, depending on policy of the individual cruise line. See also **Federal Maritime Commission Bond**.

United Nations Convention on Law of the Sea (UNCLOS)

This convention, sponsored by the United Nations, came into effect on November 16, 1994. The convention consists of 320 articles and several annexes and resolutions which establish a constitutional framework for conduct by states in the world's oceans. Among other things, it defines the extent of territorial waters, contingent zones, and continental shelf, and methods for determining boundaries. It solidifies principles of freedom of navigation, assures transit passage navigation through international straits and deals with marine pollution. Many sections concern shipping in the general sense including warships. Although a number of sections have little or no impact on cruise lines, others are quite critical, such as those that define the extent of **territorial waters**, others that deal with tribunals for law at sea, and similarly applicable sections.

Unsymmetrical Flooding

Uneven flooding across the beam or the length of the ship likely to cause a **list** or loss of **trim** if not corrected. The possibility of unsymmetrical flooding should obviously be minimized in the design of a ship, with adequate provision made for counterflooding to correct any problems that result.

Upfront Commission

Commission that is paid in advance of sailing. This is done rarely but is occasionally used as a means of encouraging sales by an agent.

Upgrade

To award a cabin in a more expensive category than that initially reserved by a passenger. This is often employed as a incentive for agents to sell cruises on an individual cruise line; as a general sales aid to help agents sell the cruise; or to confer VIP status on a passenger.

UPR

See **Unearned Passenger Revenue**.

Uptakes

Vertical pipes that carry the waste products of boiler combustion or internal combustion engine from a vessel's **machinery spaces** to the funnels for dispersion into the atmosphere. Also used for pipes that disperse excess steam. Another marine term used for these are trunks or trunking.

USCG

See **U.S. Coast Guard.**

U.S. Coast Guard

Now part of the U.S. Department of Transportation, the U.S. Coast Guard plays a crucial role in upholding safety standards in a large part of the cruise industry - that segment embarking passengers in U.S. ports. Before a **cruise ship** is allowed to take on passengers in a United States port, it is subject to inspection to ensure that it meets **SOLAS** and other international regulations regarding fire protection, firefighting and lifesaving equipment, watertight integrity and **stability,** vessel control, navigation equipment, crew competency, safety management and environmental protection. To certify compliance with **SOLAS,** the Coast Guard inspects **cruise ships** within its jurisdiction when they first arrive at a U.S. port. There are quarterly checks thereafter. Not surprisingly, cruise lines consult with the Coast Guard while design and construction is in progress. The Coast Guard may require modifications before a vessel is allowed to take on passengers at a U.S. port. Records of these Control Verification Examinations are open to the public at the Coast Guard's Marine Safety Office. USCG also seeks to enforce regulations regarding ocean dumping from U.S. vessels wherever they sail, and from non-U.S. ships within two hundred miles of the American shoreline. The Guard also monitors security provisions while ships are in United States ports. The jurisdiction of the Guard, and its influence not only on **cruise ship** design and operation, backed by **SOLAS,** is far-reaching.

V

Vacuum Toilet

The toilets that are commonly used on most modern vessels, these use vacuum suction when flushed. The process requires less water, saves weight, and functions better aboard ship. Because of the vacuum aspect, it is always recommended that guests get up before flushing, especially those who are overweight and form a more perfect seal on the toilet seat.

VDR
See **Voyage Data Recorder**.

Veranda Cabin
See **Balcony Cabin**.

Vertical Integration
Ownership or control of several travel components that do business with each other. The UK operator Airtours, which owns travel agencies, aircraft transporting passengers to **cruise ships**, and the **cruise ships** themselves; and Holland America, owners of **cruise ships** and, in Alaska, hotels and other tour infrastructure that serve as components of the integrated firms Alaska cruise and **cruise tour** business.

Vessel Sanitation Program (VSP)
Program of the U.S. Center for Disease Control that inspects and assigns sanitation ratings to **cruise ships.** Its purpose is to prevent disease outbreaks aboard **cruise ships** that are based in, or occasionally call at, U.S. **ports**. This program has substantially raised sanitation standards afloat. Not only does CDC inspect ships, it has also promulgated design recommendations calculated to improve standards of cleanliness aboard vessels. It issues what are known as "green sheets", reports printed on green paper made available to the public outlining sanitation scores of individual **cruise ships** (now also available on the Internet). Currently, 130 vessels are included in the program. Every ship carrying more than thirteen passengers and arriving in a U.S. port may be inspected. Demerits are given for deficiencies. A score of 86 out of 100 passes. The VSP was established in 1975 following several disease outbreaks aboard passenger ships. Primary focus of the VSP is minimizing the risk of gastrointestinal disease. Common areas of concern are potable water supplies, jacuzzis and pools, and the manner in which food is stored and handled prior to consumption.

Vessel Utilization Plan
A cruise line's strategic plan for vessel deployment

Void Space

during a year or season; also, the long-term plan accommodating the strategic goals of the company.

Vibration

Vibration has always been one of the most vexing challenges to the marine architect, especially during the Twentieth Century as ships have become faster and more powerful. It was a problem in the early part of the Century in the search for speed under steam. It limited the speed achievable through use of reciprocating steam machinery, and German record-breaking liners such as the *Deutschland* of the Hamburg American Line received damage from years of high-speed operation (*Deutschland* eventually had some power removed and became a full-time **cruise ship**). The legendary *Normandie*, a 1935-built record breaker of the French Line, had her afterbody extensively reconstructed following her first season of service to increase rigidity and reduce vibration. No area of design, with the possible exception of controlling smoke and exhaust emissions, has been more prone to error on the part of marine architects. Common areas of failure include lack of rigidity in **aft** structure to sustain a given speed; **propeller** design (it is not uncommon to have to replace propellers with redesigned units at enormous expense to the shipbuilder, as was the case recently with P & O's *Oriana*); and distance between **hull** and propeller. Cushioned engine mountings have drastically reduced vibration in modern **cruise ships** with diesel-electric propulsion. However, vibration problems threaten to appear once again in constructing vessels capable of cruising at 24 - 25 knots with fuel-efficient propellers.

Virtual Cruise

Cruise line marketing tool where pictures are taken aboard ship during a cruise and making them available almost immediately on the Internet. This has been used primarily by Princess Cruises in connection with the maiden voyage and Christening of *Grand Princess*.

Void Space

Empty space in the **hull** of a vessel that can often be used to store one or more of the following:

fuel, fresh water, or sea water for ballast. These spaces become an important means by which the **stability** and **trim** of a ship is maintained as fuel is expended en route and water consumed. It is also an essential element of damage control and an important means of regaining stability and trim if one or more compartments has been holed and is open to the sea because of collision, grounding, etc.

Voyage Charter
When a vessel is chartered for a single special sailing. See also **Charter.**

Voyage Data Recorder (VDR)
The maritime equivalent of the flight data recorder, or "black box", present on passenger aircraft. This is a new development not yet in general use. **IMO** is interested in seeing these provided as a means of post-accident trouble-shooting, though the **VDR** has other uses as well. Used aboard several **cruise ships,** with development led by Princess. The instrument provides such information as the ship's position, course, speed, radar information, engine orders, status of hull openings and water-tight/fire doors, monitoring of main alarms, bridge conversation including loud speaker messages given and received, ship to ship and ship to shore communication, wind speed, course, and other information. There is a built-in **Global Positioning System** which gives time and ship's location and has the capability of transmitting this information from ship to shore.

VSP
See **Vessel sanitation Program.**

VUP
See **Vessel Utilization Plan.**

W

Watch
Period of work through which some ship-board duties are assigned through a 24-hour day. The best examples are **bridge** and **engine-room** duties.

Watches are the following: 1200 - 1600: noon or afternoon watch, 1600 - 1800: first dog watch, 1800 - 2000: second dog or last dog watch, 2000 - Midnight: first watch, Midnight - 0400: second or middle watch, 0400 - 0800: morning watch, 0800 - 1200: forenoon watch.

Waterline

Although the waterline is, strictly speaking, the point reached by the water on the side of the ship's **hull** at any given time, the most visible indication of the waterline is the change in color of paint from that below the waterline to that used in the above-water hull area. The transition area, known as the "wind and water" area, two to three feet above the waterline at maximum load, is painted with special paint corresponding to the below-water color because of unusual wear and tear experienced in that area.

Waterplane

Area of water covered by a floating vessel at the waterline.

Wave Day/Week/Month

Wave day is the first business Monday following New Year's Day. Consumers, who may have been discussing vacation plans throughout the Holiday Season but not making them, begin to convert their thoughts to action the first full week of the New Year. Wave Day, and the week/month it ushers in, are often viewed as a barometer of the industry – the more intense the level of bookings during this period, the better the outlook for the year. If bookings are at less than full intensity, it is seen as a sign of recession in the cruise industry. This was regarded as a more significant indicator when the economy was in semi-recession. When the economy has continued to boom year after year, there is not as much need for indicators such as Wave Day. Articulation of the concept has been attributed to Ken Grant, former Cruise Editor of *Travel Agent Magazine*.

Ways

Before ships were built primarily in **drydocks**, vessels were constructed on the banks of rivers or at edge of harbors on the shore. When construction was sufficiently advanced so that the ship could float and be stable, the incomplete **hull** was allowed to slide into the water in a process known as a launching. Atop the bank or shore, a ship was built on a series of large rails called ways. At launching, a ship was said to slide down the ways. The moment of transition between structure-born and water-born was critical regarding stability and some vessels have foundered at launching. Once successfully launched, the ship would then be towed to a pier for final completion and fitting out.

WCISW
See **Wider Caribbean Initiative for Cruise-Ship-Generated Waste.**

Weather Deck
A deck area that is not sheltered from the sky. **SOLAS** defines this as "...exposed to the weather from above and from at least two sides."

Weather Facsimile
Electronic device that modern ships use, together with other tools, to receive forecasts of weather and sea conditions from the National Weather Service , the U.S. Navy and other organizations.

Weathertight
Dry regardless of sea state.

Weighted Average
Variously applied to a number of averages, the term is sometimes used in the industry to mean (1) the average actual availability of berths for a cruise line or the cruise industry during a year, and (2) the average number of cruise line common shares (applies to public companies only) outstanding during a specific period.

Well Deck
A small deck area, **forward** or **aft**, dropped usually by one **deck** level from the **forecastle**. Forward, this feature helped to protect the **superstructure** by breaking up waves coming over the **bow**. In both fore and aft sections, it separated this area, dominated by cargo hatches, from the passenger accommodation. Occasionally, well decks were also created **amidships**, especially when cargo holds were located there. In passenger ships of the World

War I era and earlier, the **bridge** was frequently separated from the passenger accommodation, having its own separate high-rise structure, with a cargo hatch and derricks in between. This gap was known as the "virgin's leap," since it tended to protect officers from the unwanted (?) advances of female passengers by isolating the bridge completely from the passenger accommodation.

Western Caribbean, Cruises to

Perhaps the most active cruise destination for seven-day **mass market** cruises from Continental United States, typical week-long itineraries include Key West, Cozumel, Grand Cayman, and a **port** in Jamaica. These cruises appeal to those who love the outdoors and water sports and appeal to a younger and more active clientele than sailings to the **Eastern Caribbean**.

Wet Dock

This is an increasingly common mode of vessel overhaul now that marine paints have improved to the point that it is not necessary to take a ship out of the water for bottom refinishing once each year. Wet dock periods may be used for both routine maintenance and extensive refurbishing. Typical jobs performed in wet dock: air conditioning maintenance and upgrades, changing carpets, replacement of furniture, retiling the swimming pool, and machinery overhaul. Typical maintenance pattern is a **drydock** twice every five years with some of the same functions performed at wet dock during the intervening period.

Wet Landing

Putting passenger ashore over a beach where there is no pier or other facilities for landing. For this sometimes-dangerous operation, **zodiacs** are generally used – rigid inflated rubber boats. Wet landings are a feature of expedition cruises.

Wharfage

Fee charged to move cargo or passengers across a wharf.

Wheelhouse

The specific area where the steering of the vessel takes place, normally high up and forward in the superstructure. The term is something of an anomaly, since some of the newest **cruise ships** do not have a steering wheel but are steered and controlled by means of levers. The term is often used synonymously with **bridge** and in modern ships this is correct. However, aboard ocean liners, the bridge included outdoor **bridge wings**, sometimes with enclosed observation cabs at the extreme ends. One can still see old-fashioned steering wheels aboard such ships as those of Premier Cruise Lines (*Rembrandt, SeaBreeze, Oceanbreeze, Oceanic, Seawind Crown*), aboard those of Royal Olympic, and aboard many older ships.

White Ship

(1) A ship sold or chartered to another owner or operator without name or any distinguishing marks of ownership or identity; (2) designation given by NCL to *Starward, Skyward, Sunward*, and *Southward* to distinguish these smaller ships from the blue-hulled *Norway*, a very different product.

Wider Caribbean Initiative for Cruise Ship-Generated Waste (WCISW)

A project aimed at identifying the technical and legal requirements for implementation of the **MARPOL** 73-78 convention in twenty-two Caribbean Countries. This is the most important international agreement on marine polution. The effort is supported by the World Bank and the Global Environment Fund (GEE). A major aspect of this project is to identify the requirement for waste reception facilities in Caribbean ports of call. This involves analysis of passenger numbers and routes; waste generation on board; waste treatment systems on board ships; composition of waste; amounts and types of waste and where it will be landed; recycling and waste minimization programs – all leading to the identification of future needs for handling waste at ports of call. Objective is to develop a realistic plan that can be implemented.

William M. Benkert Award

Presented by the **U.S. Coast Guard** recognizing excellence in protecting the environment on the part of operators of vessels and marine facilities. First cruise line recipient was Princess Cruises in 1998 for its programs aimed at environmental protection.

Windlass

Winch used for reeling in or releasing anchors, ropes, or cables.

World Cruise

A cruise that substantially circumnavigates the world. Such cruises are regularly offered by several cruise lines, including Holland America, Crystal, Cunard Seabourn, P & O, and others. These normally take 80-110 days, depending upon the itinerary (German lines, however, have recently offered itineraries as long as 147 days marketed in Europe). At times, these cruises will depart from the West Coast and return to the East Coast, going west-about. Although they do not completely circle the planet, they are regarded as world cruises. Indeed, this type of cruise was initiated by the Hamburg America Line before completion of the Panama Canal. Using the modern Atlantic liners *Cleveland* and *Cincinnati*, they would sail eastbound New York to San Francisco in the fall, then return westbound to New York in the winter. Had World War I not intervened, both ships would have been employed in the winter of 1914/15, undoubtedly carrying over 2000 passengers in all on world cruises. Following completion of the Panama Canal, the first true world cruise was undertaken by Cunard Line's *Laconia* in 1922. Today, such cruises can be among the most profitable and generally command the highest revenues for an individual ship in a year of cruising. However, world cruise clientele are extremely demanding in their expectation for personal service before and during the cruise. The same is true of cuisine. Costs therefore tend to be higher. However, many world cruise veterans adopt a ship and return year after year. Good examples of this: the annual world cruises of Holland America's *Rotterdam* and Cunard's *QE2*.

Although the *Rotterdam's (V and VI)* have been completely or heavily booked by those taking the entire cruise, world cruises are frequently sold in segments.

World Ocean & Cruise Liner Society
Issues the newsletter *Ocean and Cruise News*. The membership rates **cruise ships** according to amenities, cuisine, and service and these ratings are issued once each year. Editor is George DeVol.

Wrap-Around Promenade
See **Promenade Deck**.

Y

Yard Trial
A trial trip carried out by and for the shipyard, often several months before a ship is ready to undergo sea trials which are much more comprehensive in nature. A yard trial tests some of the basic engine and handling characteristics of a ship and is preliminary to the trials conducted shortly before a ship becomes the property of the intended owner.

Yeoman
Traditional designation for the position of clerk aboard a ship.

Yield
Revenues divided by the total number of available **berths**. The term is also used collectively to describe average fare levels actually collected for a ship, a cruise line, or the entire cruise industry. In the period since discounting has become quite general, this is a useful measure of the cruise industry's true profitability and demand for the cruise product.

Yield Management
(1) The art of linking fares for any given cruise sailing to the demand for it; (2) a computerized supplement to the reservation system that facilitates yield management. Such systems, currently in use by Carnival Cruise Line, Holland America, Royal Caribbean International, and Princess,

enable a line to provide for reservations agents a rate for any given cabin based on demand for that sailing. It assists management to predict, with the help of **retention forcasting**, how many passengers are likely to be aboard for a sailing at the current booking rate taking into consideration all variables. It also indicates to the cruise line the fare that should be advertised in the event the line wishes to advertise the going rate for any given sailing(s).

Z

Zodiac

Rubber inflatable boat, used aboard ships employed in **adventure cruises**, to take passengers ashore where there are no docks. This is frequently a "wet landing" experience – where landing is over a beach and passengers wear boots or get their feet wet (or both). The name comes from one manufacturer of such craft, Zodiac of France. There are many other suppliers.

notes

notes

Seatrade
CRUISE ACADEMY

The Seatrade Cruise Academy provides intensive learning for those joining the cruise industry and for executives who need to broaden their knowledge. Courses are held in Oxford, England and in key cruise industry locations worldwide.

The Academy also organises seminars and in-house training projects.

For details please contact the Seatrade Cruise Academy secretariat at Seatrade House, 42 North Station Road, Colchester CO1 1RB, UK.

Telephone +44 1206 545121
Fax +44 1206 545190
Email 100125.543@compuserve.com